MW00416797

# PRAISE FOR
## *THE SALES AGILITY CODE*

This work bridges the gap between academic theory and "in the trenches" reality. Simply put, if you create a salesforce that understands agility and knows when to change approaches, you will outperform the market ... dramatically ... and the research contained in here proves it. This goes well beyond the typical platitudes contained in most books on sales methodologies. It provides tactical, actionable, and specific strategies for dealing with nearly every sales scenario you are likely to encounter.

—ADRIAN VOORKAMP, Director, Learning Deployment, North America, Johnson Controls

*The Sales Agility Code* is a profound and thought-provoking book, focusing on the most important "f" word in sales, "fluency." This is a deep reminder to all of us that selling is an art you can learn if you can gain the right awareness of the situation you face. Read this book if you want to deploy the right knowledge and the right skills in the right way at the right time.

—OLIVER RIES, Head of Global Key Account Management and KRISHNA KALVA, Learning Solution Manager, Siemens Healthineers

Effectively ends the debate on sales methodology—one size does not fit all. *The Sales Agility Code* reveals how every seller can be agile and meet the buyer *where they are*. I found ahas in every section; your sellers will thank you—and so will your customers.

—TARIQ SHARIF, Head of Global Revenue Enablement, Talend

Sales is not for the faint of heart, and this book skillfully weaves an incredible amount of innovative content to help sellers who are committed to improvement and agility. Honestly, you've delivered the trifecta of books with *Cracking the Sales Management Code*, *Crushing Quota*, and now *The Sales Agility Code*. Well done!

—WENDY GRANTHAM, Vice President of
Sales Operations, AMMEX Corporation

This is the book that every sales and sales enablement leader should read to tackle the problem of building high-performing sales professionals. There's recognition of the need for such an approach, but there aren't a lot of books available that provide practical strategies, backed by research, to create a path to sales expertise through a focus on developing sales agility. A brilliant follow-up to *Cracking the Sales Management Code* and *Crushing Quota*.

—ANN-CHRISTEL GRAHAM, Former
Chief Revenue Officer, Talend

At first, I was a bit skeptical about this approach because I've always been a big fan of sales methodology. However, as I dug into the book, I realized that agility *is* a methodology, just not one that is rigid and procedural. Sales agility is one of our core competencies, and it's great to see a methodology centered around it!

—MARCO LAI, Director, Global Sales Operations,
for a global medical device manufacturer

This is the agile treasure chest sales teams have been awaiting for years. The authors provide sales teams with a clear picture of what it takes to implement the agile mindset and impact sales production with a flair for customer centricity. This book clearly unpacks how to put the customer at the center and focus on finding ways to increase buyer confidence through customer-centric personalized "GPS" approaches. I have no doubt by supplementing sales playbooks with the situational agile treasure chest found in *The Sales Agility Code*, you'll exceed your sales goals this year!

—KATIE KRUSHINSKIE, Global Sales Learning and
Development, Agile Coach, Dell Corporation

I have been researching sales methodologies to deploy for my field team and everything seemed too rigid, until I found *The Sales Agility Code*. Dynamically shifting our approach to meet the customer where they are is exactly what my team needs to succeed. I have been leveraging VPPs sales management framework for years and am excited to deploy that same research-backed rigor all the way to my frontline sellers.

—BOB BETZ, Senior Vice President and
Head of Sales, Pumpkin

*The Sales Agility Code* establishes the foundation for adapting in selling situations, always with an eye toward results and a focus on action. Combining data, common sense, and experience, *The Sales Agility Code* approach and training equipped our sellers to better navigate the sales situations we face. Our team is more prepared, asks better questions, and effectively serves more customers by being more "agile."

—JIM KENNEDY, Sales Leader, Ball Horticultural

Traditional sales training has long touted the universal benefits of only one song of a vast playlist. This oversimplification left sales reps to endure training that was naive by nature and arrogant in its overreaching assumptions. The authors have masterfully demonstrated that there is a time, place, and mood for every song on the list and you should learn to use them all.

What Michelle and Lisa have done is very smart and shows the grown-up thinking of researchers versus the shrill claims of generations of hacks! Your work is well documented, inclusive by nature, and allows everyone a seat at the discussion table. How refreshing in these times!

—JOHN E. DAVIS, Senior Vice President, Global Sales and Marketing, Artivion, Inc.

The authors have artfully articulated the key attributes and behaviors to elevate sales performance. They've surprised me by debunking the myth that experience equals expertise in sales. Equipping sellers to be purposeful in the development and execution of sales agility is essential as we work to elevate performance beyond gut instinct. Combining these new insights in *The Sales Agility Code* with the *Cracking the Sales Management Code* framework will produce a strong competitive advantage for our sales force.

—MARK KNUREK, North American Sales and Marketing Manager, Lubrizol

I'm very impressed with this book. It is a modern and comprehensive look at the state of sales, taking into account evolved buying habits and the need for true sales agility. It is deep on substance and models rather than just ideas. These models allow room for nuance and situational understanding that are crucial to winning with many different types of customers. *The Sales Agility Code* is one of the better books on sales I've read in the past 10 years!

—RYAN STECK, Senior Director of Sales Enablement, Henry Schein

A fresh perspective on an outdated sales approach "one size fits all," understanding the buyer's situation in all phases of the customer journey from start to finish.

—JIM FALL, Senior Vice President (retired), 3M Industrial and Safety Group

# THE
# SALES
# *AGILITY*
# CODE

**Other books from VantagePoint Performance**

*Cracking the Sales Management Code:*
*The Secrets to Measuring and*
*Managing Sales Performance*

*Crushing Quota:*
*Proven Sales Coaching Tactics for*
*Breakthrough Performance*

# THE
# SALES
# AGILITY
# CODE

## DEPLOY SITUATIONAL FLUENCY
### *TO WIN MORE SALES*

# MICHELLE VAZZANA, PhD
and
# LISA SOTTOSANTI DOYLE

NEW YORK   CHICAGO   SAN FRANCISCO   ATHENS   LONDON
MADRID   MEXICO CITY   MILAN   NEW DELHI
SINGAPORE   SYDNEY   TORONTO

1 2 3 4 5 6 7 8 9 LCR 28 27 26 25 24 23

ISBN: 978-1-264-96582-3
MHID:    1-264-96582-6

e-ISBN: 978-1-264-96965-4
e-MHID:    1-264-96965-1

The Sales Agility Code™ is a trademark of and AgileEdge® is a registered trademark of VantagePoint Inc.

**Library of Congress Cataloging-in-Publication Data**

Names: Vazzana, Michelle, author.
Title: The sales agility code : deploy situational fluency to win more sales / Michelle V. Vazzana and Lisa Doyle.
Description: 1 Edition. | New York : McGraw Hill, [2023] | Includes bibliographical references and index.
Identifiers: LCCN 2022052523 (print) | LCCN 2022052524 (ebook) | ISBN 9781264965823 (hardback) | ISBN 9781264969654 (ebook)
Subjects: LCSH: Selling. | Sales management.
Classification: LCC HF5438.25 .V393 2023  (print) | LCC HF5438.25  (ebook) | DDC 658.85—dc23/eng/20230120
LC record available at https://lccn.loc.gov/2022052523
LC ebook record available at https://lccn.loc.gov/2022052524

McGraw Hill books are available at special quantity discounts to use as premiums and sales promotions or for use in corporate training programs. To contact a representative, please visit the Contact Us pages at www.mhprofessional.com.

McGraw Hill is committed to making our products accessible to all learners. To learn more about the available support and accommodations we offer, please contact us at accessibility@mheducation.com. We also participate in the Access Text Network (www.accesstext.org), and ATN members may submit requests through ATN.

We dedicate this book to the VantagePoint team of 2022.

*We are continually amazed and grateful for the intelligence, creativity, flexibility, and integrity with which they approach every task, and the care they show our clients. Their support, patience, and belief in what we are striving to accomplish means the world to us.*

# Contents

*PART IV*
# SITUATIONAL SALES AGILITY

*PART V*
# THE PATH TO SALES EXPERTISE

# Acknowledgments

I'd like to acknowledge our data scientist Tyler Munger for working tirelessly to develop our proprietary algorithms for our AgileEdge® diagnostic process. Tyler never gave up as I continually expanded the requirements for this important process. His willingness to help with our most recent research into situational and foundational agility has allowed us to offer these significant insights for the first time to the sales training and enablement industry.

I'd like to also acknowledge Dr. Leff Bonney at Florida State University for the innovative research he and his team conducted regarding sales methodology and situational adaptation. His work was directly aligned to our research on sales management and coaching practices, and his work gave VantagePoint the starting point for validating, expanding, and operationalizing sales agility into today's sales force.

Finally, I'd like to acknowledge my coauthor Lisa Sottosanti Doyle for her dedication to VantagePoint and to the writing of this book. It has been by far the most enjoyable and rewarding writing experience I've had thus far, and I'm sincerely grateful to her.

—MICHELLE VAZZANA

I'd like to acknowledge my husband, Dan, and my children, Bobby, Matthew, and Jillian, for providing perspective and plenty of agility practice. You are each amazing and unique, and I do not take for granted how fortunate I am. I would also like to acknowledge

Michelle Dunkley for taking on more work and never once complaining and for making me laugh when I needed to vent. You are an amazing friend and colleague!

This book is better because of the VantagePoint facilitation team's willingness to share their ideas and insights. Thank you each for taking the extra time to truly partner with us. Ally Berthiaume, your guidance through this process helped me feel confident and supported. Lastly, there are many former colleagues both at VantagePoint and otherwise (Trish, Scott, Elaina, Joe, Leff, Michael, Nancy, to name a few) whose wisdom, honesty, and experience helped shape core concepts and ideas that made their way into this book. I am grateful to each of you.

—LISA SOTTOSANTI DOYLE

# Introduction: The Death of the One-Size-Fits-All Approach and the Birth of an Agile Era

Every sales author claims to share the "one best way" to sell that is far superior to all others. You've likely read at least one book on consultative selling. Perhaps another on developing an effective value proposition. Yet another on value selling. The landscape of sales experts is vast. If you are reading this book, you have most likely been through several sales training programs that have claimed to be the best. You likely took something useful out of each one, but none of them were revolutionary.

This search for the best way to sell has befuddled salespeople and sales leaders for years. And now we know why: research has revealed that a one-size-fits-all approach to selling is doomed to fail. In fact, any given sales approach has been shown to be effective approximately 25 percent of the time.[1] The best salespeople do not use one set path. They choose a path based on the buying situations they face.

*Sales agility* is defined as the ability to assess and make sense of the situation an individual is facing, choosing the best path forward aligned to the situation, and then planning and executing the chosen path. In a nutshell, sales agility represents good decision-making that leads to effective execution in sales and other domains.

This will be the first book to detail the decisions the best sellers make as they navigate sales opportunities. In other words, we will explore how salespeople understand what is unique about the buyers' situations, how they select the best sales path forward, and how they execute this approach to increase the chances of a win. We won't make bold claims based on our own experience as super sellers. We will share real research based on what real high-performing sellers do and how to replicate it.

The purpose of this book is to disrupt conventional wisdom regarding sales effectiveness and sales enablement. For over 50 years, sales and learning leaders have attempted to find the best sales methodology to implement with their sales force. And for over 50 years, this approach has tied the hands of sellers and irritated potential buyers. These attempts at standardization are crippling today's salespeople because they don't reflect the reality of the buyers they face, reducing the percentage of sellers at quota by more than 20 percent.[2] By focusing on sales agility, sellers can get a more accurate read of their buyers' situation, select the strategy that is most likely to lead to a win, and dramatically improve overall performance. Our research at VantagePoint confirms that sales agility is the most accurate representation of high-performer behavior.

In this book, we will share what we have learned through VantagePoint's extensive research. We are committed to performing challenging research, asking the hard questions, and getting inside the nitty-gritty details so that salespeople and sales managers can embrace and deploy effective sales agility. Our quantitative studies of high-performing salespeople and sales managers have teased out the nuances that separate the best from the rest. We will detail the scope and findings of this research in Chapter 2. VantagePoint takes these insights and builds frameworks to replicate what high performers do day in and day out. These frameworks translate to step-by-step processes for equipping sellers to embrace sales agility to improve sales performance.

Our bestselling books *Cracking the Sales Management Code: The Secrets to Measuring and Managing Sales Performance*[3] and *Crushing Quota: Proven Sales Coaching Tactics for Breakthrough Performance*[4] have revolutionized the way sales managers manage. We've taken the very complex job of sales management and made it accessible to everyone. Because of our research and our findings, sales managers now have a simple, yet powerful way to ensure that their sellers are executing the right activities, to coach those activities to ensure effective and consistent execution, and to assess leading indicators of success. As an important extension to that work, we are revolutionizing the way salespeople sell.

Organizations across the globe have benefited from our research and highly executable frameworks. And you can too. When you consume and apply the content of this book, you won't have to worry that you are being sold the next best idea. Our research findings are outlined inside this book, and they are accessible to you. You'll learn the implications for agile selling and some executable frameworks for selling all based on what we've uncovered about how the best salespeople win more sales.

What might surprise you is that it is not overly complicated. While many other sales frameworks and methodologies are very complex, we offer the minimum effective dose. Why? Because simplicity matters. More is almost never better, certainly as it pertains to sales and sales management. Just ask busy salespeople if they'd like one more sales tool. They will run away quickly. Very quickly!

When we say "simplicity matters," we are not implying that selling is easy. In fact, we acknowledge that it is a very hard profession with almost unlimited nuances. What we know from our research and experience is that better decision-making leads to better execution. And the best salespeople are disciplined decision makers. Period. They favor conscious choices over quick assumptions, which helps them avoid the traps that ensnare other sellers.

Salespeople who are agile don't wait until they have all the answers before moving forward. They gather enough information to make informed decisions, and then they act. They don't let the desire for perfection paralyze their selling efforts. This doesn't mean they are hasty. In fact, the most successful salespeople spend more time initially assessing their buyers, making a logical approximation of what they are facing, choosing the approach that fits, and then executing. What this means is that they are more likely to make good choices and not have to backtrack and fix costly mistakes.

The highest-performing salespeople have mental models that help them narrow the field of play, reducing unnecessary complexity in their opportunity pursuit. This allows them to make the sales task more manageable by putting it into bite-sized chunks and not overcomplicating it. As sales expertise increases, it becomes simpler for these high-performing sellers to make and implement effective decisions. The assessment and decision-making process becomes part of their sales muscle memory. The mindset of simplicity doesn't mean execution is easy. It means that execution is aligned to the situation.

The highest-performing salespeople aren't just great decision makers using mental models. They also have a growth mindset. Research has revealed that high performers in every domain have a similar mindset. In her groundbreaking book *Mindset: The New Psychology of Success*, Dr. Carol Dweck revealed that there are two primary mindsets: *fixed* and *growth*.[5] A *fixed mindset* indicates that people believe they are who they are and they're not going to change much. A *growth mindset* indicates that people believe they can change and grow. Growth mindset people are insatiably curious. They are not afraid to try new things because they are not afraid of failure. They see stumbles as necessary parts of growth, and they learn from each experience.

In our interpretation, agility requires a growth mindset. To be agile, you have to be continually refining your thinking and your sales approach based on changes in the buyer situation. A growth mindset indicates that improvements can be made and performance can be improved. It requires salespeople to resist the idea that, "Wow, I finally got this. I don't need to learn anything new." Our approach to sales agility embodies the growth mindset by equipping salespeople to continually question their assumptions, rethink their approach, seek advice and insight from others, and never settle into one way of doing things. In this book, we will examine the elements of an agile mindset and why this mindset and associated curiosity (an indicator of a growth mindset) are necessary ingredients for mastering sales agility.

Another interesting research finding on top performance in every field is that there is almost no correlation between experience and expertise.[6] This is true in all domains, including sales. Just because salespeople have been selling for 20 years or more, it does not make them an expert. Salespeople who become experts behave differently. They challenge assumptions, reach outside of their comfort zones, and find new and more effective ways to sell. Throughout this book, we will disclose the path that the highest-performing sellers follow to turn experience into expertise.

So, the question is, are you ready? Are you ready to consider that one-size-fits-all selling is a myth? Or that today's informed and complex buying teams will not tolerate salespeople who try to force fit a sales process onto their buyer's journey? Are you ready to demystify the complex job of selling and enjoy higher win rates and more satisfied buyers? Are you ready to approach your sales job with a growth mindset and rethink your approach? If so, let's begin.

# PART I

# DEBUNKING THE MYTH OF THE "ONE PERFECT SALES METHODOLOGY"

## CHAPTER 1

# Chaos Is the New Normal

## BUYERS ARE EVOLVING

In recent years there has been a significant shift in how buyers approach buying. Consider what happens in a typical day: We turn on our smartphones, and the notifications are tailored to us. We go on Facebook, Snapchat, or Instagram, and we see ads directly related to our preferences. Our news feeds are filtered by our viewing history. In essence, we experience a unique world, designed specifically for us. This spoils us, increases our desire for highly relevant information, and lessens our tolerance for sorting through information we see as "noise." These personal experiences are shaping us as buyers and creating a world of hurt for salespeople.

Technology has rewritten the sales game both directly and indirectly. The most significant direct impact of technology is that it has made available *a lot* of good-quality information for both buyers and sellers. The plethora of available information complicates the task of buying and selling in meaningful ways. Indirectly, this explosion of information has created confusion and a shift in how buyers buy and what they want from salespeople. Few sales organizations ignore the direct consequences of technology, but it is the indirect consequences that have the most significant impact. Those who choose to ignore the indirect consequences of the technology revolution, particularly buyer confusion, do so at their own peril.

The net effect of these highly curated personal buying trends is that buyers are more informed than ever before in ways that are highly relevant to their wants and needs. At the same time, buyers are less available. They don't see a need to reach out to a salesperson because much of the information they want can be obtained via websites and other informational sources. In earlier times, salespeople were the keepers of product and solution expertise. Those times are long gone. Industry analysts at Forrester estimate that 67 percent of the buying journey is done digitally.[1] This creates a conundrum for sellers because buyer thinking is being shaped by sources other than the salesperson.

## BUYERS WANT INSIGHT

Buyers are no longer satisfied with product or service pitches. They know about your products and services because they've examined your website. They've most likely read analyst reports that evaluate your company against competing alternatives. According to Gartner research, customers are awash in high-quality, credible information.[2] Improvements in data analytics, content thought leadership, and sales messaging have resulted in high-quality information that informs most business-to-business purchases.

You are probably thinking that this high-quality information is of enormous benefit to the buyer, right? Wrong! Again, according to Gartner, an overabundance of high-quality information is hindering the buyer's ability to make good purchase decisions. Why? Because 44 percent of buyers report encountering various information sources with contradictory claims. This supposedly trustworthy, yet conflicting information affects sellers negatively, reducing the chance of making a high-quality sale by 66 percent.

It is hard for buyers to sort through what is good information and what is just noise. Buyers must learn to be more discerning about what they learn online, more critical of information. Ultimately, buyers are looking for the truth, but that truth often seems elusive, cloaked in opinions and positions that may lack validity. Buyers need to evaluate evidence, not just claims made by sellers and marketers. Many claims made by slick sales messaging are appealing, but they are not based in fact. The assertion that more information is better is false. Better information is better.

Think about the last time you purchased a smartphone. You most likely got a quick-start guide as well as a link to the user manual. How many of you go beyond the guide and dig into the manual? My bet is that not many of you explore or read about the nitty-gritty details of the device you bought. Having more features does not make the phone better, especially if you don't care about them. As you skim user manuals, you encounter information that matters to you and information that doesn't. Likewise, during the buying journey, buyers pivot and change in big ways throughout their process as they react to information and changing conditions.

What does this mean for you as a salesperson? It means that you must focus on finding ways to increase buyer confidence and help the buyer prioritize the information that matters. The most successful sellers help their buyers make sense of the barrage of information they encounter, creating confidence and reducing skepticism. This sense-making approach builds a feeling of control in the mind of buyers, helping them interpret information and make high-quality, low-risk decisions.[3]

## TRADITIONAL SALES ENABLEMENT EFFORTS ARE FAILING

In the past, salespeople believed that solution expertise was the key to sales success. If I know my product thoroughly, understand the competitive landscape, and understand the customer's needs, I'm good. This leads to organizational efforts that map out the steps required to successfully sell their product or service and equip salespeople accordingly. Most organizations strive for a standardized approach to selling. Intuitively, this makes perfect sense. A standardized approach makes it easier to develop and support a diverse sales force. For many large organizations, this standardization is seen as the key to scalability and growth.

Yet, this approach is no longer sufficient. Buyers demand personalization. Solution complexity continues to increase, making it nearly impossible for sellers to attain and maintain "expertise" in everything they sell. And because markets change so frequently, making sales enablement decisions to map the "right" path is often futile. Sellers need a better way of managing through the chaos of an overinformed world.

The problem is not with *what* sales enablement has been trying to do but in *how* it has been done. The desire for standardization makes sense because it promotes scalability and growth. Unfortunately, all too often, the wrong things are standardized. The focus had been on standardizing the selling process and not standardizing how we interact with the buyers on their journey. Sales enablement teams focus enablement efforts on "taking buyers on the sales journey," not joining the journey the buyers are already on. Buyers are rarely interested in a seller's process. They are laser focused on their own wants and needs.

Buyers want sellers to evaluate their environment, scan the marketplace, and come to the table with an educated, valid point of

6

view. This is not the same as an opinion. Buyers want a logical, practical analysis of their situation, a synthesis of available trends and market data, and a comparison of options that narrows the scope of their decision. The goal of this effort on the part of the salesperson is intended to simplify their buying task and build confidence in their decision.

## THE OVERENGINEERING PROBLEM

Most large organizations adopt a particular sales methodology as a way of standardizing their sales process, ensuring rigor and discipline in the way sellers execute. They aim to provide their sellers with a map that can help them travel smoothly from qualification to closing. As part of this process, many sales leaders select the methodology that they feel best meets the needs of their sales force. Most commercially available sales methodologies are designed to work in a wide variety of circumstances, pretty much in *all* circumstances. Considering the marketplace chaos, the rate of change, volume of information, and unique buyer needs that sellers face in the pursuit of deals, it begins to seem shortsighted to believe that one sales methodology is enough.

The reality is that these rigid methodologies don't work well in any circumstance. In fact, the highest-performing salespeople are the least likely to adopt a standardized methodology.[4] The best sellers know that they must flex what they do to address the buyer's circumstances.

Salespeople need options—different strategies for different situations. They do not need a map that becomes outdated almost as soon as it is finished. Actually, they don't need a map at all. They need a GPS. While maps detail what the landscape looked like at the time they were drawn, a GPS flexes to the current conditions. Maps are outdated tools for today's sales world. Sellers need to be able to adeptly navigate the congested and evolving buying landscape and determine the most effective path to take to succeed.

## LEANING INTO THE NEW SALES REALITY

The reality that a seller-centric, highly engineered, one-size-fits-all approach doesn't work is a hard sell for many sales organizations. It flies in the face of past experiences. Even the thought of figuring out how to equip salespeople to be flexible versus following a standardized process is bewildering. Going against traditional approaches can feel risky and uncomfortable. It can feel like you're trying to buck the tide.

We had one of our clients acknowledge that one-size-fits-all approaches don't work, agree that salespeople need to be agile, and then become paralyzed by the implications for sales enablement efforts. The task of allowing for variation and agility seemed too big. This same client acknowledged they knew that by standardizing on a methodology, they were marginalizing salesperson effectiveness. The change seemed too big. It is a harsh reality when leaders feel they must select mediocrity because it is easier to implement. The good news is that it is far easier to lean into agility than leaders think. The bigger risk is holding tight to something that research proves doesn't work!

Technology has changed everything and has forced a rewrite of the sales game. The volume of information available to both buyers and sellers is overwhelming. Buyers approach sales differently and are more skeptical of salespeople. Buyers who feel more confident in the information they consume make bigger and bolder purchase decisions. The market shifts quickly and sometimes unpredictably.

A new dynamic is afoot that we can't ignore. Let's not pretend that the marketplace is going to revert to the way it was. This is the new reality, and it requires a different set of skills to succeed. Persistence and assertiveness are the table stakes. Leaning into the chaos requires persistence and assertiveness *plus* the ability to discern, move quickly, and not rest on the success of past actions. The next shift is coming quicker than we think.

The agility needed to navigate this rapidly changing landscape is a new frontier, requiring a different mindset and different approach. Using traditional approaches in a vastly different sales environment is a recipe for failure. We can acknowledge that standardization is desirable, but it is effective only if we standardize the right things. The sales process should mirror the steps buyers take to acquire your solution, not just the steps sellers must take to sell the solution.

So, how do we determine what should be standardized? How do we know what works and creates satisfying buying experiences and sales success? We do our research. We do our homework. We actually study high performers in depth to understand what they do and why they do it. We gather evidence. The good news is that there are patterns in how buyers behave that can be understood and applied by sellers to reduce friction in the buyer's journey and create better alignment between buying and selling efforts.

## THE IMPORTANCE OF EVIDENCE

Far too many sales training companies rely solely on case studies to "prove" the efficacy of their methodologies. They train to their specific methodology and look for evidence that it worked. In far too many cases, researchers design studies to support conclusions they've already reached. This approach to research falls into the category of confirmation bias. We believe this approach is backward and more than a bit self-serving. Effective researchers study high-performing individuals, isolate the patterns and behaviors of high performers, and develop frameworks to replicate high-performer behavior. This is true in all domains, not just sales.

---

**They train to their specific methodology and look for evidence that it worked. In far too many cases, researchers design studies to support conclusions they've already reached.**

---

We are not suggesting that case studies are ineffective. We use them as well, primarily because they are interesting and paint a story of what a buyer might expect. The downside of relying exclusively on case studies is that they don't require research and they typically only involve one company. How do you know that the case study results hold true across multiple and varied organizations? How do you know if the methodology you are getting ready to adopt is the right one? How do you know if it is truly reflective of what high-performing sales managers and salespeople do in the real world? This is where it gets tricky.

In addition to an examination of the impact of a particular methodology, you may want to understand the methodology's genesis. How was it derived? When? With whom? These are the hard questions that buyers have the right to ask and have answered to make the most informed sales training and enablement decisions.

Our passion for research and intense curiosity about what separates the highest performers from the rest of the pack allows us to offer practical insights for sales enablement efforts. We hope this deep dive into *sales agility*, and the importance of evidence-based frameworks, will help purchasers of sales training become more informed and discerning consumers of sales training and enablement solutions.

Due to increased attention being paid to sales agility, it is time to put a stake in the ground, shared a research-based definition, and detail the impact sales agility can have on sales execution. In the next chapter we will unpack extensive research into the behavior of high-performing salespeople and sales managers. We will discuss how sales agility manifests within sales organizations and what that means for effective sales execution. We will also discuss how the world of sales has changed and what the most successful salespeople do to succeed in this new reality.

## SUMMARY

Buyers are evolving. Personal buying experiences that are curated and tailored to the individual are changing our preferences and expectations of how we buy in a business context. In addition to increased desires for personalization, buyers are now faced with increasingly large amounts of relevant, high-quality information. Buyers struggle to make sense of this information in ways that aid their purchasing decisions. Buyers want insight. They want to know how the information they access is relevant to their buying decision.

Traditional sales enablement efforts that drive standardization are often focused on seller behavior rather than buyer behavior. Many of these efforts result in an overengineered selling process that binds the hands of sellers and creates frustrating experiences for buyers. The most successful sellers are agile, and they are the least likely to adopt a procedural, standardized approach. Evidence points to the need for agility to aid sellers in effectively navigating continually changing buying landscapes.

Organizations that embrace agility must seek and verify evidence that any approach to agility is truly reflective of high-performer behavior. This evidence-based approach reduces ambiguity and builds confidence in sales enablement and training decisions.

## KEY TAKEAWAYS

- Personal buying experiences are shaping the way buyers think about purchase decisions, making them demand more curated, personalized buying journeys.

- Technology is driving a surge in the amount of high-quality information available to our buyers. Much of this information is conflicting, which confuses buyers and reduces the chances of making a high-quality, low-risk buying decision by as much as 66 percent.

- Buyers expect sellers to provide insight, beyond product and services. They want sellers to look across the marketplace, pay attention to changing trends, evaluate information from the buyers' perspective, and help them narrow the scope and simplify their buying journey.

- Traditional sales enablement efforts toward standardization are crippling the sales force because the buying landscape is constantly changing.

- Many sales training programs are designed as a one-size-fits-all approach intended to work in any situation. These methodologies tend to be overengineered, and they are not applicable to today's real buying and selling environments.

- Agility is the approach favored by high-performing sellers and sales managers, acknowledging that buying and selling are situational. The right approach depends upon the situation.

## CHAPTER 2

# The Three Levels of Sales Agility and the Sales Agility Research Journey

When we set out on this research journey, our intent was to study high-performing sales managers and salespeople and figure out which behaviors separated the best performers from the rest of the pack. The humbling thing about being committed to research is that the researchers must be willing to be wrong and have their hypotheses disproved. That's what happened to us. So, we continued to search and re-search, and through that process we have uncovered some powerful findings that have the potential to dramatically affect the way sales leaders equip their salespeople and their sales managers.

Our initial hypothesis was that we would find the one best way to coach and manage and, we hoped, the best way to sell. We didn't expect that agility would be the common theme. However, time and time again, we found that the highest-performing sales managers and salespeople approached their tasks situationally. They adapted the way they approached their jobs to align to the situation they faced. This may seem obvious now that we point it out; however, it is not the way sales managers and salespeople are typically trained.

To sort out the findings and the implications for selling and managing, we began our journey by defining what sales agility means and how we know. There were common themes that emerged across the many research studies.

## SALES AGILITY: SURPRISING AND POWERFUL THEMES

In our research studies spanning 14 years, we identified some common themes that held true for peak performance. These themes continually emerged and led us down a different path than the one we anticipated:

- Sales management and sales are both situational.

- There is no one-size-fits-all approach to effective selling or effective coaching.

- Effective decision-making is a prerequisite for effective selling and coaching.

- The best decisions lead to the best execution.

- Most sales and sales coaching programs focus on execution and overlook the necessary first steps of critical thinking and decision-making that form the heartbeat of sales agility.

## THE PUNCHLINE: AGILITY IS SITUATIONAL

As we continued to plug away at our research, an amazing thing happened. A pattern started to emerge that held true with each study. Agility is situational. But what does that mean? How do we define a situation?

Well, it depends. The key theme in our research is that the best path forward "depends" upon the situation an individual (the buyer) is facing. If a seller or sales manager can get a proper read on the buyer's situation, the decision-making and subsequent execution improve dramatically. Agile salespeople and sales managers exhibit the following pattern of behavior that sets them apart from their lower-performing peers:

1. *Assess the situation.* In this step sellers and sales managers seek and evaluate information to get an accurate read and make sense of the situation they are facing.

2. *Choose the best path forward.* For both sellers and sales managers, the connection between potential actions and situational factors points to which behaviors and actions will be most effective based on the situation they face.

3. *Execute the selected actions effectively.* Sellers and sales managers *monitor* the impact as well as the continued changes in the situation.

---

**If a seller or sales manager can get a proper read on the buyer's situation, the decision-making and subsequent execution improve dramatically.**

---

Researchers with the Gartner firm, which specializes in "business growth strategy for sales leaders," call this process a combination of situational awareness and situational tuning and propose that situational selling is the most effective approach to use to navigate complex buying journeys and add value to the buying experience.[1] If the most effective selling is indeed situational, what types of situations do salespeople and sales managers face, and what types of decisions do they need to make to improve sales execution and maximize performance?

The first and most important point to clarify is that agility is a multifaceted phenomenon within the sales force. In fact, we identified three primary levels of sales agility that exist within the sales force. Each level of sales agility requires different, yet related, decisions to drive effective execution. Frameworks are provided for the decisions that must be made that affect execution at each level of sales agility. See Figure 2.1 for the three levels of sales agility: *organizational*, *situational*, and *foundational*.

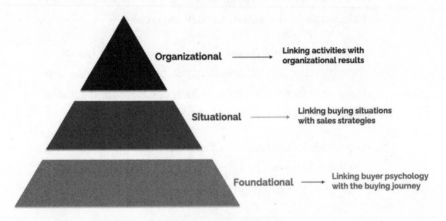

**Organizational** → Linking activities with organizational results

**Situational** → Linking buying situations with sales strategies

**Foundational** → Linking buyer psychology with the buying journey

FIGURE 2.1 **Levels of Sales Agility**
*Source:* VantagePoint Performance.

We will unpack these levels, starting at the top with *organizational agility*. Although it is true that effective organizational agility matters, it is primarily the domain of sales managers and sales leaders to execute agility at this level. If you are interested in becoming a sales manager or leader, organizational agility will matter to you. Even if you don't aspire to sales leadership, it is helpful to understand what your leaders do that assists your selling efforts.

## ORGANIZATIONAL AGILITY AND THE SEARCH FOR THE ONE RIGHT WAY TO COACH AND MANAGE SALESPEOPLE

VantagePoint conducted four large-scale studies to examine how the most successful companies measure and manage their sales force. As a salesperson, the way you're managed is highly relevant because it affects your daily life. Our first study of sales metrics revealed that there was no one best way to measure sales performance. Rather, sales metrics fell into three primary categories: business results, sales objectives, and sales activities. In addition, activity coaching was the only type of sales coaching in our studies that was positively correlated to quota attainment. High-performing managers coached less frequently but for longer durations than their lower-performing peers. This alignment between salesperson activities, sales manager coaching, and organizational outcomes forms the basis of organizational agility.

The first, and often overlooked, series of decisions high-performing sales managers make involves the alignment of organizational goals to frontline sales execution. Whenever change happens either in organizational direction or marketplace realities, the ability to survive and thrive boils down to what happens at the frontline level. This scares the heck out of sales leaders, and for good reason.

---

**Whenever change happens either in organizational direction or marketplace realities, the ability to survive and thrive boils down to what happens at the frontline level.**

---

No matter how effectively leaders strategize, the execution of those strategies rests on the shoulders of frontline sales managers and salespeople. That's a hard reality, but it is true for every sales organization. What happens at the front line determines success or failure. So how do you ensure that salespeople are executing the right things, in the right way, and at the right time to achieve organizational goals? You embed organizational agility in the hearts and minds of your frontline sales managers. This additional guidance on the importance of connecting field-level execution to organizational results does not organically occur just because you promote your top salespeople to sales management. Salespeople tend to favor the needs of the customer over the needs of their own organization.

*Organizational agility* is the clear and specific alignment of organizational goals (results) with targeted key performance indicators (KPIs)—that is, sales objectives—and high-impact salesperson activities. Which activities have the greatest impact and are the most important? It depends. It depends upon the results you're targeting, which KPIs you need to move, and which activities you must consistently execute well, which metrics need to move in the right direction.

This alignment is key because circumstances will change, and when they do, organizations, and sales managers specifically, need to identify how to adjust their focus and how to make strategic decisions about which activities will accomplish their new objectives and ultimately achieve results. The decision about which activities sellers must execute, how, and when became the *first critical component of our organizational agility framework.*

To figure out which activities sellers must execute, start backward at your desired destination, as shown in Figure 2.2.

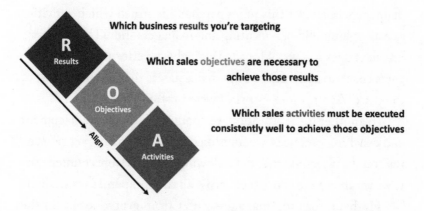

FIGURE 2.2 **Connecting Results, Sales Objectives, and Sales Activities**
*Source:* VantagePoint Performance.

This first set of decisions, those that align organizational goals with frontline execution, answers the question, "What should my salespeople be doing?" It is one of the most important decisions sales managers can make, and it is one that sets up their sales team for success. The ability of sales managers to make the critical decisions about how to focus seller effort equips organizations with the agility to adapt quickly and effectively to change. You can find detailed descriptions of our findings about organizational agility in our bestselling book *Cracking the Sales Management Code: The Secrets to Measuring and Managing Sales Performance.*[2]

This alignment of activities to results is just the first in a series of three critical decisions that drive effective sales execution and organizational agility. The next major decision a sales manager must make is to determine what to coach, how to coach, and when to coach sellers to ensure execution happens according to plan.

The next step in our organizational agility journey was to explore how to coach for maximum impact. Of all the things sales managers could coach, what should they coach? That is often a daunting choice. At this point, we had identified which activities salespeople should be executing and managers should be coaching. The next question was, How do the highest-performing sales managers coach to activities in ways that separate them from the rest of the pack? Again, more surprises were in store for us.

In another in-depth study we conducted of sales management and coaching practices, we identified some surprising, yet refreshing trends. It seemed that the following patterns were counterintuitive, yet they were consistent across all the companies we studied.

High-performing managers differ from everyone else in the following ways:

- They coach fewer hours per month per seller (approximately three to five hours per month).

- They coach less frequently.

- They coach for longer durations.

- They cover fewer topics, in more depth.

- They are more formal in their coaching approach.

- They spend less time in the field.

- They are significantly less likely to use scheduled coaching time for inspection and forecasting.

You can find a detailed description of the findings of this study in our book *Crushing Quota: Proven Sales Tactics for Breakthrough Performance*.[3] We know that the best-performing sales managers orient selling and coaching efforts to those activities that matter most. How do they do it? Figure 2.3 depicts the essence of the most powerful and agile sales coaching.

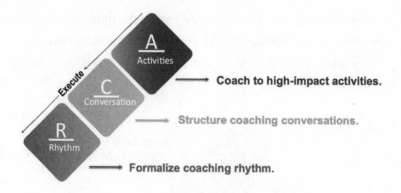

FIGURE 2.3 **How Agile Sales Managers Coach**
*Source:* VantagePoint Performance.

The highest-performing sales managers structure their coaching conversations for maximum impact, orienting coaching toward deeper discussions of fewer topics. They have agendas, inputs, and outputs. They provide this coaching within a formal coaching rhythm. They do not overcomplicate this; they formalize only the things that matter most. This second decision in the organizational agility framework answers the question, "How can I best enable my salespeople?" It is the codifying of the manager's role in driving the right kind of sales execution.

The third and final element of the organizational agility framework involves ensuring that sales and coaching efforts are having the desired effect. The most agile sales managers monitor leading indicators to assess whether the right needles are moving in the right direction. Are close rates improving? Is the pipeline full of the right types of deals with the desired types of customers? If yes, business as usual. If not, adjustments must be made to ensure continual alignment between organizational goals and field-level execution.

This final decision about which leading indicators are moving in the right direction answers the questions, "Is it working?"

or, to be more specific, "Are sellers executing the right things in the right way, being coached effectively, and having the desired impact?" Figure 2.4 depicts the three primary decisions that enable organizational agility.

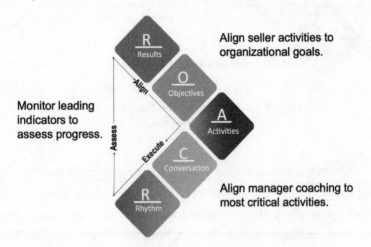

FIGURE 2.4 **Framework for Organizational Agility**
*Source:* VantagePoint Performance.

Now that we've distilled the research and practices around organizational agility, we'll turn our attention to our powerful research on salesperson agility, starting with situational agility.

## SITUATIONAL AGILITY AND THE SEARCH FOR THE PERFECT SALES METHODOLOGY

The next series of studies originated with the Florida State University (FSU) Sales Institute.[4] We became aware of these studies via VantagePoint's involvement in a sales leadership summit held at Harvard University. One of our former colleagues was impressed with the innovative research shared by the FSU Sales Institute's director at that time. A series of research studies was conducted to answer an important question: "Is there one best sales methodology, and if so, is it the Challenger Sale?"[5]

In 2012 the Challenger Sale[6] was spreading like wildfire, and sales leaders wanted to know if it was the new best way to sell. It was markedly different than prior consultative sales approaches in that it was more seller-out focused rather than customer-in. Sellers using this challenging approach came to customer conversations prepared to disrupt typical buying patterns with new insights. This disruptive approach is discussed in more depth in Chapter 11.

The first study in the series was an attempt to replicate the original challenger study conducted by the Sales Executive Council. The researchers at FSU wanted to find out (1) if the Challenger Sale was real, and if so, (2) if it was the best methodology available on the market. The findings were consistent with the original study and confirmed that high-performing salespeople were much more likely than average and low performers to self-identify as challengers. The surprise was that high-performing sellers were just as likely to self-identify as consultative sellers as they were to identify as challengers.

Even though the researchers at FSU were able to replicate the initial challenger research, they still had no answers regarding which methodology was the best on the market. The second study was initiated after one of the research participants in the first study mentioned that he had had a hard time answering the survey questions. He said that the survey asked him what kind of seller he *was*. The answer he wanted to give was not reflected in the survey instrument. He said, "I utilize all of these approaches (challenging, relationship, consultative, problem solver, and so on) depending upon the situation I'm facing."

This caused the researchers to ask different questions. "Do high-performing sellers adapt their approach to different buying situations, and does that lead to higher win rates?" This was a much more interesting set of questions, and it came closer to pinpointing which methodologies mattered most. The researchers gathered data on sales approaches used by sellers in three different companies. Salespeople were presented with three types of buying situations that were industry relevant. In Figure 2.5 you can see what the researchers found.

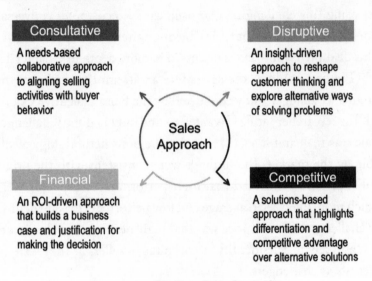

### Consultative

A needs-based collaborative approach to aligning selling activities with buyer behavior

### Disruptive

An insight-driven approach to reshape customer thinking and explore alternative ways of solving problems

### Financial

An ROI-driven approach that builds a business case and justification for making the decision

### Competitive

A solutions-based approach that highlights differentiation and competitive advantage over alternative solutions

**Sales Approach**

FIGURE 2.5  **The Four Sales Strategies**
*Source:* VantagePoint Performance.

High-performing sellers displayed four different patterns of selling, moving between these strategies as the situation dictated. Average- and low-performing sellers stuck to the same strategy regardless of the buying situation they were facing, and it was typically the methodology they'd been trained to use. This was a troubling finding. Think about the implications to sales enablement efforts. When organizations launch a one-size-fits-all sales methodology hoping that it will create standardization and improve performance, they are unwittingly training their sales force to behave like their average and low performers.

High performers are least likely to adopt and use a standardized methodology. Why? Because that's not the best way to win more deals. High performers do what works, not necessarily what they were trained to do. The second important finding was that when high-performing sellers switched between different strategies based on the situation they faced, this adaptive behavior led to higher win rates.

In addition, none of the four strategies (consultative, disruptive, competitive, and financial) emerged as a clear leader. So, the answer to the question "What is the best sales methodology?" is, "It depends." There was no clear winner. There was not a "best one" approach. The best approach depended upon the specific *buying situation* the seller was facing.

> **High performers do what works, not necessarily what they were trained to do.**

Figure 2.6 highlights the following conclusions:

- On average, salespeople face between four and six types of buying situations. These types of buying situations reflect five to seven specific buying factors that most significantly predict adaptive salesperson behavior.

- High-performing sellers select the most effective of the four sales strategies to align to the buyer and increase the chances of a win.

- Average- and low-performing salespeople use one primary strategy in all buying situations, and it is typically the one they were trained to execute.

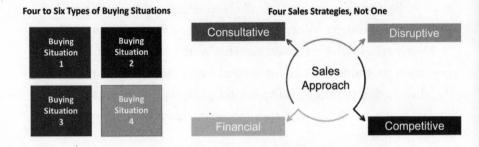

FIGURE 2.6  **Buying Situations and Sales Strategies**
*Source:* VantagePoint Performance.

We sought to validate the FSU findings and attempted to replicate their results. We were able to validate their findings (see the Appendix for research details); however, in our continued quest for evidence-based sales frameworks, we had more questions that needed to be answered. One important question was whether there were patterns within the 25 buying factors that could help sellers simplify the task of making sense of each buying situation.

By interrogating a large data set, we discovered two important things:

- Of the buying factors in the FSU study, 8 rarely occurred and were removed from the larger set, reducing the total number to 17. This was extremely important for data analysis purposes, and it increased the reliability of the output.

- The 17 buying factors fit into five categories (see Figure 2.7), which was far easier for sellers to understand and examine. It was easier for salespeople to get their head around gathering five different types of information versus 17 individual factors.

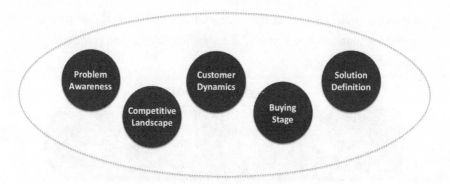

FIGURE 2.7  **The Five Categories of Buying Factors**
*Source:* VantagePoint Performance.

The conclusion we reached was that orienting seller effort toward only five buying factor categories was a more practical approach to situational agility, and it could be replicated. An understanding of these five buying factor categories enabled high-performing sellers to make sense of any buying situation they faced and select which of the four primary sales strategies was most likely to lead to a win. But we didn't stop there. We had more questions and sought more answers on the nature of sales agility.

## FOUNDATIONAL AGILITY AND THE EXAMINATION OF WHETHER CONSULTATIVE SELLING IS DEAD

When we analyzed the buying factors across 4,192 buying situations, one buying factor, the buying stage of initial engagement with the salesperson, was significant in all the buying situations we studied across all companies. This was the only buying factor that was consistently important and relevant, and we gained a new, deeper appreciation for the importance of the buying journey and the buyer's stage within that journey. It appears we uncovered a foundational factor that had a dramatic impact on the nature of buying situations See Figure 2.8 regarding the buyer's stage within the buying journey.

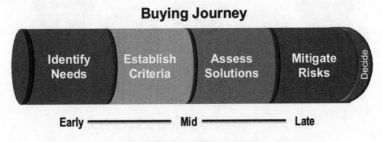

FIGURE 2.8 **The Buyer's Stage Within the Buying Journey**
*Source:* VantagePoint Performance.

This finding was not surprising. An understanding of the buyers' stage within their buying journey is critical for several reasons. First, where the buyers are within their buying journey changes as they progress from stage to stage. Decision science informs us that people are generally risk averse and are twice as likely to make a change to avoid pain rather than achieve gain.[7] This is especially true early in the buying journey when the buyers have not yet determined if a change is warranted.

Once the buyers move beyond the ambivalence about whether to change, their perspective moves toward one of gain—that is, how they stand to improve by making a change.[8] We explore buying stage and the buying journey more extensively in later chapters. For now, we turn our attention to the four sales strategies and how they relate to one another.

## FOUR SEPARATE SALES STRATEGIES OR NOT?

The next question we sought to answer was how the four sales strategies (consultative, disruptive, competitive, and financial) related to one another. Was this distinction as discrete as the FSU team believed, or was it more nuanced? Also, we sought to find out whether consultative selling was truly a discrete pattern or more highly correlated to the other three strategies. Due to our finding that buying stage was a foundational factor, our hypothesis was that consultative selling was a launching point in the execution of any of the other strategies.

As indicated in Figure 2.9, the consultative selling tactics were highly correlated with the tactics within the other three strategies. So, in response to the question "Is consultative selling dead?," the answer is a resounding no! Consultative selling is alive and well, and it is foundational to being able to execute any of the other strategies. In addition, the use of the consultative tactics was high regardless of the primary strategy selected, meaning that sellers executed heavy use of the consultative tactics even when they chose disruptive, competitive, or financial as their dominant strategy.

FIGURE 2.9 **How the Four Sales Strategies Align**
*Source:* VantagePoint Performance.

We also discovered that when a salesperson was engaged early in the buying journey, the use of consultative selling tactics was *six times higher* than if the salesperson was engaged late. This higher use of consultative tactics early versus late was replicated in two separate studies.

Since consultative selling is a critical component of sales agility, it warrants further discussion about what it is. Confusion abounds regarding (1) what consultative selling is, and (2) if it is the same as basic sales skills. Through our research, we found that an effective consultative selling program must include the following elements to enable foundational agility:

- Foundational sales skills such as call planning, opening, questioning, positioning capabilities, closing, and objection handling.

- Buyer psychology and the buying journey. Because the buying stage within the buying journey is so significant, salespeople need to understand how buyers navigate that journey, what their goals and motivations are at each stage, and how to align seller behavior accordingly.

- Effective call planning for conducting sales calls at different stages of the buying journey. Early-stage calls are more about discovery and identifying buyer problems and needs. Mid- and late-stage calls are about differentiation and helping the buyers make sense of various alternatives.

## WHICH CONSULTATIVE TACTICS MATTER MOST?

We were curious to know which one of the consultative tactics was most predictive of wins. Again, we were surprised at what we found. Our hypothesis was that uncovering needs would be the most predictive tactic. This seemed intuitive, and it aligned with our own selling experience. However, it turned out that obtaining incremental commitments along the buying journey was the consultative tactic most highly predictive of wins. This has significant implications for consultative selling. It means that when planning individual sales interactions across the buying journey, a very intentional focus on gaining commitment at each stage matters. A lot.

Any planning process should begin with the end in mind and work backward. Salespeople have a much better chance of gaining incremental commitments if they identify them ahead of time and put together a cohesive plan for the sales call that includes seeking and sharing information relevant to the desired outcome. This makes sense in everyday life as well. When you get in your car, you map out your route based on your desired destination. This idea of beginning with the end in mind is the same approach as we find with organizational agility: starting with desired results, linking to objectives and KPIs, and selecting the sales activities that are most strongly aligned.

The most important aspect of foundational agility is to understand how buyers buy, what motivates them at each stage, and how to plan and execute sales conversations differently at different stages. If salespeople don't understand the fundamentals of a buying journey, it is highly unlikely that they can understand that different buying situations involve different buying journeys. Again, there is no one-size-fits-all approach to foundational agility or consultative selling. How a seller plans and executes the best sales calls depends upon where the buyers are within their buying journey.

---

**The most important aspect of foundational agility
is to understand how buyers buy,
what motivates them at each stage, and
how to plan and execute sales conversations
differently at different stages.**

---

# SUMMARY

The net outcome of the research studies indicates that the most effective approach to both managing and selling is situational. *Situational fluency*—or the ability to adapt and execute effectively in various situations—is at the heart of all three levels of sales agility. Sales managers must coach and orient seller behavior to the most important activities that drive the desired organizational results. Managers must continually evaluate leading indicators to determine if the right needles are moving in the right direction. Having the agility to make real-time adjustments helps ensure that field-level execution is aligned with organizational priorities. This approach to sales management and coaching enables true organizational agility.

The highest-performing salespeople are agile. They exhibit four different patterns of sales behavior and flex between those patterns depending upon the existing situation. They seek and make sense of a variety of buying factors to tease out the buying situation they face, choose the sales approach that has the best chance of a win, then execute the appropriate tactics, constantly monitoring buyer reactions and changes in the buying situation. This approach forms the heart of situational agility.

Consultative selling is more than just one of the four sales strategies. It is a foundational set of skills that equips sellers to assess the buyers' location within their buying journey, determine buyer motivations and objectives, and then plan and conduct sales calls differently at different points along the buyers' journey. This flexing of the sales approach and aligning seller behavior to the buying journey forms the basis of foundational agility. In the following chapters, we will do a deep dive into the nature of foundational agility.

## KEY TAKEAWAYS

- Research into high-performing sellers and sales managers yields surprising results, often conflicting with conventional wisdom.

- The best, most agile sales approach is based on recent research of high-performing sales behavior, indicating that the most agile sellers adapt their sales approach to match the situation they face. Only average and low performers use the same approach regardless of the existing situation. And that's what they've usually been taught: one approach . . . one methodology!

- Effective selling and effective sales management are both situational, and decision-making is a powerful prerequisite for all types of sales agility.

- The most agile sellers and sales managers incorporate the following steps of sales agility:
    - Assess the situation.
    - Choose the best path forward.
    - Execute the choice, and monitor the impact.

- Organizational sales agility ensures that frontline manager execution is directly tied to key performance indicators and desired results.

- Situational sales agility ensures that salespeople are accurately assessing and making sense of the buying situation, choosing the sales approach with the highest chances of a win, executing the selected tactics, and monitoring buyer reactions.

- Salespeople face between four and six different types of buying situations and display four common patterns of sales behavior.

- Foundational sales agility acknowledges that the buyers' location within their buying journey is a necessary predecessor to sales strategy selection.

- Consultative selling is foundational to sales agility, forming the basis by which sellers choose alternative paths according to the existing buying situation.

- Consultative tactics are used highly regardless of the primary sales strategy selected.

- Obtaining incremental commitments along the buying journey is the tactic most highly correlated to wins, meaning that any effective planning process should begin with the desired outcome and work backward.

# PART II

# FOUNDATIONAL SALES AGILITY

## CHAPTER 3

# Getting into the Buyer's Mindset

## YOU KNOW YOUR CUSTOMERS HATE TO BE SOLD, RIGHT?

Why do buyers hate to be sold? It doesn't seem intuitive. If you are in the market to buy something, you most likely expect to deal with an individual who is selling what you want to buy. However, we don't typically behave in rational ways. We are often resistant to help even when we need it. What do you do when a retail salesperson asks if you need help? You most likely say, "Thanks, but I'm just looking." This is an almost automatic response. We've done it so many times that it seems like second nature. We say it even when we *are* looking for something specific.

We like to buy. We just don't like to feel like we're being sold. What does it mean to "be sold"? Feeling like we are being sold means that we are feeling pressured—manipulated—into doing something someone else wants us to do. When we feel manipulated, we tend to emotionally disengage or become angry or frustrated. This leads to a breakdown in collaboration and active engagement. When this happens during sales conversations, sellers often sense this disengagement, but they don't always know what to do about it. As salespeople, we want to bring value to our buyers, so having a thorough understanding of how buyers think, how they behave, and how they buy is critical to building value in our selling efforts.

An unfortunate reality is that most sales calls result in very little perceived value to the buyer. First, it is useful to examine the reason buyers and sellers communicate at all. In addition to sharing information, we communicate to motivate and influence each other's behavior.[1] This is certainly true in sales. The primary job of a salesperson is to sell stuff. To effectively sell a product or service, the salesperson must influence the buyer's behavior. The seller must move the buyer from a position of uncertainty about change to a desire to change. Yet, buyers are resistant to salespeople. In our personal and business buying experiences, we often see salespeople as pushy. We want to avoid them whenever possible.

Perhaps this is because many sellers lack an understanding of how buyers buy. Although buying has become more chaotic and complex, there are some predictable things buyers do as they navigate their buying journey. The goal of any purchase is to make the best possible purchase decision. Prospects are often looking to gain the most, spend the least, and experience long-term satisfaction with their purchase. Sellers can help buyers find these solutions if they are familiar with buyers' psychology.

## BUYERS LIKE THEIR OWN IDEAS MORE

First, sellers need to know buyers are often conflicted about change. They identify reasons to change, as well as reasons not to change. It is the job of the salesperson to tip the scales in favor of change. This is where the magic happens in sales. The degree to which the seller motivates the buyer to move beyond the status quo and toward change determines the success or failure of selling efforts. Why is this task of motivating buyers to change so difficult?

Buyers, and humans in general, like their own ideas. They are invested in them. The most effective salespeople plan and conduct conversations that enable buyers to talk themselves into changing based on their own values and interests. Unfortunately, this is not the way most sales calls unfold. Why? Because most of us are help-ers. We're problem solvers by nature. We see a problem, and we want to solve it. In fact, this style of problem solving often manifests as a rather directive style of selling. We ask questions to understand buyer needs, and as soon as we uncover problems we can solve, we offer solutions. We don't do this to be annoying. We do this to be helpful. It just doesn't have the effect we want.

This problem-solving orientation is called the *righting reflex*.[2] It occurs when a salesperson is motivated to help prospects solve problems. The rub is that just because buyers have a problem doesn't mean they are prepared to solve it. Ironically, this desire to help, to solve problems, often has the opposite effect on buy-ers. Buyers may want to change, or more precisely feel that they should change, and yet they don't want to change at the same time. Change is hard, change is complicated, and it is unknown. No mat-ter how flawed the status quo is, it is known. A buyer's ambivalence is often a roadblock for a salesperson.

When we attempt to motivate our buyers to change, buyers are psychologically hardwired to take the alternative position. When sellers orient dialogue toward change, buyers often mentally shift to all the reasons why they should maintain the status quo. When *we* (salespeople) suggest change and the many reasons why change is warranted, we generate resistance. Buyers dig in their heels and defend the opposing position. This is completely counterproductive to influential and effective selling, and in many cases, it does not serve the needs of the buyers.

So why does this happen? Because most humans trust their own opinions more than those of others. The further your idea (or solution) is from the other person's ideas, the more resistance you will likely meet. There is an expression that captures this phenomenon: "We don't argue with our own data."

If you as a salesperson are advocating for change, your buyer is most likely oriented against it. People don't like to be told what to do, even if it is in their best interest. Case in point: If a friend tells me I need to lose weight, I'm not happy about it. I feel that they are butting in. I'm likely to shut down or disengage. If *I decide* I want to lose weight, I'm much more likely to take corrective measures regarding diet and exercise. I'm willing to eat healthier if it is "my idea." I'm willing to exercise more often if it is "my idea."

The biggest challenge for salespeople (and therapists and coaches) is that it requires patience and skill to change another person's ideas. Let's use therapy as an example. An experienced therapist likely has a good idea of the patient's problems within the first session or two. It is also likely that the therapist knows what the patient needs to do differently to address the problem. So, why doesn't the therapist say something like, "Let's cut to the chase. I've sorted out your problems. If you want better relationships with your family, you must create and maintain healthy boundaries. Here's how you do that."

A good therapist would never do that. Why? Because the therapist is not the one who needs to change. It is the patients whose behavior needs to change. The therapist needs to help them discover the need for change themselves, define what change is possible, and articulate the benefits of taking action.

What does this mean for sales? It means that buyers, like all people, learn about their own attitudes and beliefs in the same way others learn them: they learn by *talking* about their attitudes and beliefs. The tricky part is *how* buyers talk about their own attitudes and behaviors matters. A lot. This is where emotions come into play.

---

It means that buyers, like all people, learn about their own attitudes and beliefs in the same way others learn them: they learn by *talking* about their attitudes and beliefs.

---

## BUYERS ARE EMOTIONAL CREATURES

Humans are emotional beings. They make emotional decisions and find rational reasons to justify them. It is very appealing to lean into logic and rationality when selling. It seems obvious that if the buyers have a problem, they should want to solve it. Many sellers have scratched their heads when they make a rational business case why a buyer should make a change, and the buyer does nothing. Deals stall, and it doesn't seem to make sense. It only makes sense when you consider the relationship between the elephant and the rider. According to Jonathan Haidt, professor of social psychology at the New York University's Stern School of Business, emotions and rational thought are like an elephant and a rider (Figure 3.1).[3]

The elephant represents the buyer's emotions. The rider represents the buyer's logical, rational mind. It shouldn't surprise you that since the elephant is much larger than the rider, the elephant will do what the rider wants only if the elephant *wants* to do it. The elephant is bigger and stronger than the rider and ultimately has the control.

FIGURE 3.1 **The Elephant and the Rider**
*Source:* Adapted from Jonathan Haidt, *The Happiness Hypothesis: Finding Modern Truth in Ancient Wisdom* (New York: Basic Books, 2006), pp. 3–5.
Image copyright © bswei/123rf.com (www.123rf.com).

Our emotions are bigger and stronger than our rational mind. As salespeople, we tend to appeal to the rider and ignore the elephant. We appeal to logic over emotion. We do this at our own peril. As salespeople, we need to improve our skill at understanding and exploring our buyers' emotions related to change. Once buyers have emotional reasons to change, they are much more likely to act.

Which emotions should we tap into with our buyers? Again, this is where psychology of decision-making comes into play. According to Daniel Kahneman, prolific researcher and recipient of the Nobel Peace Prize in Economics, people are twice as likely to act to avoid pain rather than to achieve gain.[4] Loss aversion is a very, very powerful force, and bad information is processed more thoroughly than good information. Let's review a few scenarios to make this point more concrete. Considering Figure 3.2, you have two choices, A and B. Which choice would you make?

## Which Choice Would You Make: A or B?

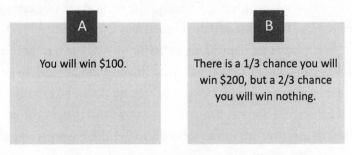

FIGURE 3.2 **Which Choice Would You Make: A or B?**
*Source:* VantagePoint Performance.

If you are like most people, you will choose A because it is a sure gain and it lets you avoid potential loss. Choice A also feels safer, making it an emotional choice. Choice B is a more rational option since you could have won more, but it felt risker because of a potential loss.

Let's look at this same choice framed differently. Consider options C and D in Figure 3.3. Which would you choose?

## Which Would You Choose: C or D?

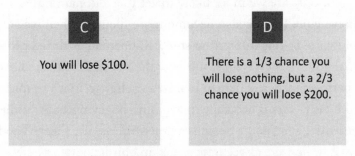

FIGURE 3.3 **Which Would You Choose: C or D?**
*Source:* VantagePoint Performance.

Most people choose option D. Why? Because option C is a guaranteed loss. With option D, you might lose more than $100,

43

but you might lose nothing. If you examine the two examples, they are the same but worded differently. The second set of examples reflects a *loss-frame* rather than a *gain-frame*.

We exhibit more risk-taking behavior to avoid pain rather than achieve gain. Change often feels risky. Buyers (and humans in general) make changes when the pain of staying the same exceeds the pain of change. This pain avoidance is a powerful insight for salespeople. In essence, our job as sellers is to get the buyers to explore the downsides of not changing in very tangible ways. We need to make the downsides of not changing concrete and real. We need to do this *before* we start exploring the upsides of making a change. This act of exploring and clarifying potential pain is very motivating to our buyers, even if it feels a bit unnatural to us as sellers. Pain drives action.

---

**Buyers (and humans in general) make changes when the pain of staying the same exceeds the pain of change.**

---

Not only are we more likely to act to avoid pain rather than achieve gain, but we also become more focused when we act to avoid pain. In one interesting study, Kahneman analyzed professional golfers, their scores, and how their accuracy affected overall performance. Kahneman looked at golfer accuracy in making birdie putts versus accuracy in avoiding bogey putts. A birdie is a potential gain, and a bogie is a potential loss. In Tiger Woods's heyday, if he were as accurate at making birdie putts as he was in making putts to avoid bogeys, his average score would have gone down by an entire stroke, and he would have made on average $1 million more per year.[5]

Pain and gain both matter in decision-making, but gain without pain is not very motivating and rarely leads to action. Now that we know buyers are emotional and make decisions primarily for emotional reasons and then find rational justification for those decisions, let's layer on the journey that most buyers follow when they do decide to change.

## THE STAGES OF THE BUYING JOURNEY

Buyers go through a series of stages when they make large decisions, both in their personal and professional lives. The easiest way to think about a buying journey is that buyers do different things early, mid, and late in their journey (Figure 3.4).

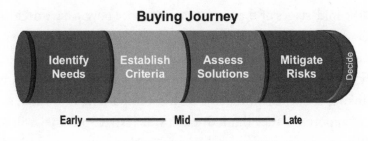

**Buying Journey**

Identify Needs · Establish Criteria · Assess Solutions · Mitigate Risks · Decide

Early ——————— Mid ——————— Late

FIGURE 3.4 **The Buying Journey**
*Source:* VantagePoint Performance.

### The Early Stage: Identify Needs

In the early part of their buying journey, they identify problems they are facing and determine whether those problems are worth solving. This early stage of the buying journey is critical because the degree to which buyers are motivated to change drives their behavior throughout the rest of their buying journey. If buyers never mentally and emotionally decide to fix their problems, the journey ends. This decision to change or not to change is a big one, and it is something salespeople often get wrong.

If we hearken back to the ambivalence buyers feel about change, we know that they have reasons to change and reasons not to change. Just because the problems are big doesn't mean buyers have decided to address them. The buyers must be the ones to make the decision to change, not the salespeople. Pipelines are full of bad deals that are stalled because buyers are not willing to make a change. Whether a change is warranted or logical doesn't matter. Change is a big step, and the decision to change is the biggest hurdle buyers must overcome in their buying journey.

## The Mid-Stages: Establish Criteria and Assess Solutions

In the mid-stages of the buying journey, once buyers have decided change is warranted, their mindset shifts from a problem orientation to more of a solution orientation. Buyers begin to identify what is important to them in making a change. Buyers begin thinking about which criteria are most important and which are least important. They think through which trade-offs they will be willing to make. Buyers *establish criteria* they will use to evaluate alternative solutions.

Once the criteria are established, solutions are evaluated. Buyers *assess solutions* to determine the degree to which they fit the needs and criteria the buyers have established. As buyers evaluate different solutions, their buying criteria can and often do change. New criteria emerge while others fall off the list. The buyers begin to narrow down what is most and least important, as well as which solutions are the best fit.

## The Late Stage: Mitigate Risk

Finally, in the later stages of the buying journey, buyers shift their thinking from what they will gain by making the change, to potential risks and downsides of making a bad decision. Buyers want to feel good about making the change, and they want to eliminate any potholes or risks that could occur. They typically want to talk to references to determine efficacy of their chosen vendor. They want to ensure that the terms of the sale are favorable. The goals at the late stage are to *mitigate risk*, and they want to ensure that the terms are favorable and contingencies have been considered.

In summary, once buyers have decided in the early stage of their buying journey to do something to solve their problems or improve their situation, they begin to decide what it is they want. During the middle stage, they develop criteria they use to evaluate different alternatives. Once they have a sense for what is most important and least important to them, they look at various solutions. They weigh the relative fit of different solutions to their requirements, and they narrow the playing field down to their final choices. Finally, in the final stage of the journey before they decide to act, buyers examine the potential risk associated with the solution. They look for ways that the decision could go wrong, and they also look for ways to minimize the chances of a bad decision. Once they have effectively mitigated their risks, they make their decision.

## THE BUYING JOURNEY IN ACTION

We mentioned that this buying journey is relevant to both our business and personal decisions. Let's use a common decision many of us make to illustrate the buying journey in action. Imagine you have decided to buy a house. As with many decisions, dissatisfaction with your current situation has been the primary driver. The urban apartment you have been living in was great when you first moved in. It was close to work and to nightlife, and it was not too big to keep organized and neat. However, your situation has slowly changed over time. A few years ago, you got married, and now you have twice as much stuff to fit in the same amount of space. At first the crowded conditions felt cozy, but now a few years and one dog later, it has been feeling pretty cramped. Nevertheless, even though it has not been ideal, it has still been manageable.

Now a baby has come along. Your apartment is supercrowded, and it is bursting at the seams. The urban setting that you loved as a newlywed couple is no longer as important. The apartment has begun to feel like a bad fit. Although it was perfect when you rented it, it isn't meeting your current needs. You've decided the status quo is no longer sufficient, and you are ready to make a change. You've decided it's time to move, to buy a house, and to have more room for everyone.

The next series of decisions you face involve determining what is important in a house. You know you need more room, but how much room? How many bedrooms and bathrooms do you want? What location seems desirable? Do you need a garage? Do you want to be close to family? What is your price range? What style of house appeals to you? You must answer all these questions before you can begin a meaningful search for a house. Why? Because when you search online for houses or speak to a real estate agent, the answers to these questions allow you to evaluate relevant options. Online real estate platforms require users to input specifications. Real estate agents ask for these same specifications. Once your criteria have been developed, you can look for a house.

Now you are actively searching for the right house. In many cases, the criteria you developed change. You realize that your initial budget will not get the house you desire. You must adjust your criteria or raise your price point. In addition, new criteria may emerge. You may realize that the size of the yard is more important than you originally anticipated. You want to have a deck and a playset for your child. You look at house after house until you narrow it down to the top one or two choices. You are close to making an offer, but you need to do some due diligence to ensure that you are making the best decision.

In the later stages of the home buying journey, you may dig deeper to determine if the area is as desirable as you anticipated. You do some research on the schools in the area. You examine the crime levels and trends. You probably look at insurance prices in different areas as well. All this information helps you mitigate any fear or risk you feel in making this decision.

Once you've decided on a house and signed the contract, you're still not done. You order a home inspection to evaluate the condition of the house you are preparing to buy. You find out what is wrong with it and how bad it is, and you decide whether you are still prepared to move forward with the sale. In many cases, you ask for concessions from the seller to address any issues revealed in the home inspection. Only after these steps have been taken and any issues resolved are you ready to go through with the home purchase.

This simple personal example shows clearly how we make decisions. It is true in our personal and professional lives. First, we navigate the challenges we face and determine if they are big enough to fix. If our problems warrant fixing, we start determining what we want in a solution, which things we must have, and which things we can do without. Prioritization is important and helps us narrow down the scope of possible solutions.

Once we have a clear sense of what we want, we can explore alternatives. As we explore alternatives, new needs emerge, and requirements can change. We then narrow down our choices to arrive at our top choice. At that point, we set about finding ways to reduce the risk in making our decision. We want to make a change, and we know what we want. However, we don't want to make a mistake. This important step of reducing our risk allows us to make our decision with confidence and reduces the likelihood of experiencing buyer's remorse.

## SUMMARY

We explored the fact people like to buy, but they don't like the feeling of being sold. Pushy or overly assertive behavior from salespeople can cause buyers to dig in their heels and defend the status quo. Buyers like their own ideas better than those of salespeople, and buyers don't argue with their own data. Because of this orientation, it is imperative for sellers to make it the buyers' idea to change, which requires both skill and patience.

Buyers are emotional beings who make emotional decisions and find rational reasons to justify them. Salespeople mistakenly believe buyers will buy simply because the sellers have made a solid, rational business case for change. However, many stalled deals in salespeople's pipelines attest to the error of this belief. As salespeople, we tend to rely too much on logic and too little on the emotional content of our sales conversations. Emotions come in the form of pain due to problems and concerns as well as desires to improve the situation. Pain is a much more powerful motivator, particularly in the early stages of the buying journey. Buyers are twice as likely to make a change to avoid pain than they are to achieve gain. This means that buyers must see the pain of staying the same—or maintaining the status quo—as bigger than the pain of change.

Buyers go through a predictable series of steps when making buying decisions. This is true in our personal and professional lives. We consider whether we need to change, decide what we want, determine who can best provide it, and find ways to reduce our risk. Then we decide.

This deep understanding of buyer behavior, and how that behavior changes across the buying journey, forms the key capability that enables foundational agility. In the next chapter, we will explore how the most agile salespeople leverage this understanding of buyer behavior to align their selling efforts to win more sales.

## KEY TAKEAWAYS

- Buyers are human beings and therefore subject to fundamental aspects of psychology. They resist overt attempts at influence and manipulation.

- Buyers like their own ideas better than salespeople's, resulting in the need to make purchase decisions the buyers' ideas.

- Buyers are hardwired to make emotional decisions, and then they find rational reasons to justify those decisions.

- Buyers are more than twice as likely to take action to avoid pain than they are to achieve gain.

- Buyers have different motivations and objectives at different stages of their buying journey:
  - Early stages are focused on identifying needs, understanding problems and desires, and determining whether a change is warranted.
  - Mid-stages are focused on establishing which criteria are most important in making the buying decision and assessing the viability of alternative solutions.
  - Late stages are focused on mitigating risk and ensuring that proper terms are met.

- Large decisions in our personal lives mirror similar elements of the buying journey.

CHAPTER 4

# Assessing the Buying Situation

In the preceding chapter, we examined the nature of buyers. We explored how they behave and why they behave that way. In this chapter, we explore the core decision-making framework that reflects *foundational sales agility* in action.

Although our research revealed that consultative selling was foundational to all four sales strategies, not all consultative selling approaches reflect sales agility. We will tease out the differences between a procedural approach to consultative selling and an agile approach to buyer-seller interactions. Our goal in this chapter is not to teach the totality of a consultative selling approach but to explore the elements of consultative selling that represent the most important components of foundational sales agility.

We indicated in Chapter 2 that understanding the buyers' journey and being able to ascertain the buyers' location within that journey is foundational to sales agility and effective consultative selling. Understanding buying stages is important because the buyers' mindset changes as they navigate each stage of their buying journey.

To that end, Figure 4.1 reflects the powerful decision-making framework we will use to (1) assess where buyers are within their buying journey, (2) choose and plan our sales interactions to align to the buyers' journey, and (3) effectively execute our plan. In this chapter we focus our efforts on the *assessment step*, and how this important first step lays the groundwork for better choices and better execution.

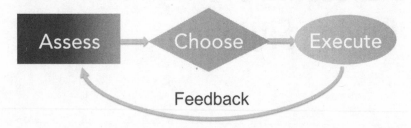

FIGURE 4.1 **Assess, Choose, Execute**
*Source:* VantagePoint Performance.

What we assess, the choices we make, and how we execute change across the stages of the buyers' journey. We pay particular attention to the early and mid-stages of the buyers' journey because that is where foundational agility is most critical.

## ASSESSING FOUNDATIONAL BUYING FACTORS

In our overall agility research, we identified five categories of buying factors that must be considered when assessing the buying situation. Foundational agility incorporates three of the five buying factors within the assessment stage. In Figure 4.2, you see the three primary categories of buying factors that must be assessed, as well as what information is needed to conduct an effective assessment.

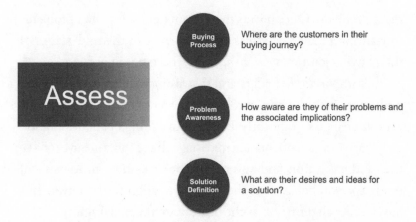

FIGURE 4.2 **Assessing Foundational Buying Factors**
*Source:* VantagePoint Performance.

In Figure 4.3, you can see how the buying factor categories are reflected at different stages of the buyers' journey. The *buying process* category reflects the overall buying journey. The buyers' level of *problem awareness* is critically important to understand and influence, particularly in the identify needs stage of the buying journey. The level of problem awareness affects whether the buyers will move beyond consideration of problems and express a desire to fix

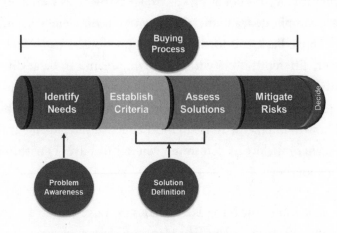

FIGURE 4.3 **Buying Factors and the Buying Journey**
*Source:* VantagePoint Performance.

those problems. Once buyers move from examining their problems to wanting to act to address them, moving to the mid-stages of their buying journey, *solution definition* becomes important.

It is important to understand this distinction between early and mid-stages in the buying journey because buyer objectives and motivations change significantly. Buyers move from a pain orientation early stage to a gain orientation mid-stage. These shifts in buyer objectives and motivators and buyer behavior necessitate an adjustment in salesperson behavior if the seller is to align to the buyer. This buyer-seller alignment is at the heart of foundational agility.

> This buyer-seller alignment is at the
> heart of foundational agility.

## ASSESSING BUYERS' LOCATION WITHIN THE BUYING JOURNEY

Although understanding the buyers' location within their buying journey is vital, it is not always as straightforward as we'd like. Buyers are complicated, and their journey is not completely linear. They often move back and forth revisiting previously made decisions. In fact, different buyers within a buying team can be at different points along the buying journey. Exploring the details of the buying journey helps us determine what is important to the buyers and how to interact with them most effectively. Read and evaluate the scenario below to determine where this buyer is within their buying journey:

> *Scenario 1:* The buyer is a logistics manager within a manufacturing plant. The plant supervisors have received a variety of noise complaints from the workers in the offices

surrounding the production line. Apparently, the noise levels are distracting and impeding productivity of the administrative staff.

The plant manager has explored this issue and feels that the noise complaints are valid. The plant manager has tasked the logistics manager with finding a solution to reduce noise in the administrative area.

The logistics manager has researched noise-reducing options online, has found a few potential solutions that wouldn't require a significant construction project, and has identified a few companies that offer these low-disruption solutions. The logistics manager has secured a meeting with a salesperson from QuietTech, one of the potential vendors.

So, is the logistics manager in the early or mid-stages of their buying journey? First, we must consider the level of problem awareness. What is the degree to which the logistics manager is aware of the noise problems? Have the size and scope of the problems been examined? In answer to these first few questions, it seems that the noise complaints have been properly vetted and appear valid. The productivity of the administrative staff has been affected, and a solution to the noise problem is warranted. This buyer has already navigated the identify needs stage of the buying journey.

How about solution definition? Are there any specific requirements indicated for a potential solution? A low-disruption solution is one of the requirements. The plant manager has indicated that he does not want a big construction project and is seeking a solution that doesn't require major changes to the building's construction. Therefore, we have at least one requirement identified, although more requirements must be considered.

Since the logistics manager has already evaluated the noise problem, vetted the problem and found it to be serious, and even researched low-disruption solutions, the logistics manager is in the mid-stages of the buying journey, specifically the assess solutions stage. This manager is actively seeking solutions and looking at vendors. It doesn't mean that this sale is a sure thing. What it does mean is that this buyer is highly likely to purchase a noise reduction solution, whether from QuietTech or another vendor.

Now let's evaluate another scenario and tease out the buyer's location within their buying journey:

> *Scenario 2:* The buyer is a plant manager at a medical manufacturing plant. She attended a conference last week on advances in manufacturing practices and ran into her old friend the logistics manager (from scenario 1). They caught up on recent events, and they even chatted about the noise problem the logistics manager recently addressed.
>
> This piqued the plant manager's interest to learn more about whether some of the same issues were afoot within her own plant. Employee productivity is very important in all manufacturing plants, and hers was no exception.
>
> The logistics manager passed on the name and contact information of the plant manager to the QuietTech salesperson. The salesperson reached out and scheduled a conversation with the medical manufacturing plant manager for the following week.

Let's examine the plant manager's location within their buying journey. Is the plant manager actively seeking noise reduction solutions? No. At this point, the plant manager is looking to learn more details about what is currently happening within her plant. Although she has agreed to meet with the QuietTech salesperson, no specific noise reduction solutions have been considered.

How about problem awareness? How aware is the plant manager at this point about noise problems in her medical manufacturing plant? It appears an evaluation of potential noise concerns has not yet occurred. The plant may or may not be experiencing noise problems, and it has yet to be determined. Due to the lack of problem awareness, it is likely that the plant manager is at the very *early stages* of a potential buying journey, the identify needs stage.

Low levels of problem awareness are associated with the early stage of the buying journey. The plant manager may or may not have noise problems, and a solution may or may not be warranted. The salesperson has a very different task in this scenario versus the task in scenario 1. In scenario 1, the logistics manager was actively looking for a solution to thorny noise problems. In this scenario 2, the plant manager is curious to learn more about the work her friend did with QuietTech; however, she is nowhere close to seeking a solution.

## USING QUESTIONS TO ASSESS THE BUYERS' POSITION IN THE BUYING JOURNEY

Not all buying situations are as straightforward as these two scenarios provided. It is the job of the salesperson to tease out information about the buyers and the buyers' situation. Questions are a necessary tool sellers use to gain relevant information about their buyers. We offer a simple, yet powerful questioning model in Figure 4.4 to assist sellers in gaining the needed information to determine the buyers' location within their buying journey.

You'll notice this questioning approach consists of three primary types of questions: (1) *background questions* to uncover details and context of the buyer's situation, (2) *pain questions* to uncover and clarify buyer problems, and (3) *gain questions* to understand buyer needs and desires to address identified problems.

FIGURE 4.4  **Questions to Assess the Buyers' Position**
**Within Their Buying Journey**
*Source:* VantagePoint Performance.

*Background questions* help answer the question, "What's going on here?" Background questions are very useful in seeking information about steps the buyers have taken thus far in their buying journey. Have the buyers done an analysis of their current situation? Have they started to identify any criteria or requirements that must be met? Have they looked at a variety of potential solutions? Answers to these questions will help the salesperson get a read on where the buyers are within their buying journey.

*Pain questions* answer the question, "Do problems exist, and how bad are they?" And *gain questions* examine the degree to which buyers want to solve their problems and answer the question, "Are these problems big enough to fix?" While background questions are neutral, pain and gain questions examine the emotional context of the buyers' situation. Because we make decisions for emotional reasons and find rational reasons to justify those decisions (as we discussed in the previous chapter), the use of pain and gain questions is a very powerful tool in the agile salesperson's toolbelt.

> *Pain questions* answer the question, "Do problems exist, and
> how bad are they?" And *gain questions* examine the degree
> to which buyers want to solve their problems and answer the
> question, "Are these problems big enough to fix?"

In Figure 4.4, you'll notice that the three types of questions, background, pain, and gain, are not depicted in a linear fashion. Many consultative selling methodologies advocate a specific sequence for asking discovery questions. Most methodologies advocate a pain-first questioning approach, taking the position that uncovering problems is necessary prior to exploring desires for a solution. Our research and experience invalidate the usefulness of this sequential approach, indicating that agile sellers change the way they use questions to align to the buyers' situation and different stages of the buying journey.

## USING QUESTIONS EARLY IN THE BUYING JOURNEY: ASSESSING PROBLEM AWARENESS

In the early stage of the buying journey, the buyers have not yet decided to act. In this case, a pain-driven approach to questioning is most appropriate. Buyers are twice as likely to act to avoid pain than to achieve gain. This is especially true early in the buying journey, when buyers are asking themselves, "Are these problems big enough to fix?" The size of the pain and the level of the buyers' problem awareness are directly related to whether the buyers will move forward in the buying journey or abandon it all together.

Figure 4.5 indicates the use of background, pain, and gain questions. You'll notice that the arrow indicates the use of background questions, then pain questions, followed by gain questions.

This pattern is particularly effective when buyers are early in their journey, in the identify needs stage, and undecided about whether change is warranted.

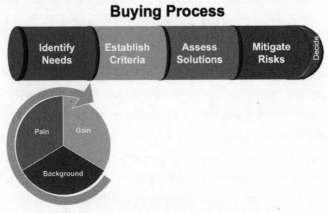

FIGURE 4.5 **Using a Pain-Driven Approach**
*Source:* VantagePoint Performance.

Once a salesperson has uncovered and clarified the buyers' problems and the size and scope of those problems, it is then appropriate to begin using gain questions to explore the upside of solving problems and improving the buyers' situation. A very common failure point early in the buyers' journey is for sellers to shift to gain questions too early and seek buyers' opinions about solving their problems.

Remember, people change when the pain of the status quo exceeds the pain of change. Without sufficient problem awareness, buyers are unlikely to act. Stalled deals are the result. The best use of questions shifts meaningfully as buyers progress along their buying journey.

## Sample Pain-Driven Approach

*Background question:* What piqued your interest in speaking with me about noise reduction for your plant?

*Pain question:* Have you received any noise complaints from your administrative employees? If so, tell me more about them and the nature of the complaints?

*Pain question:* How has this noise problem affected your employees' ability to focus their efforts? Are they having to roam around trying to find a quiet place to work?

In this scenario, once noise problems have been uncovered and explored, it would be useful to shift to gain questions to determine if the plant manager has an interest in exploring solutions to the noise problems:

*Gain question:* If you were to reduce the noise and distractions for your administrative staff, how would this affect their productivity?

This shift from pain to gain questions moves the buyer closer to wanting to act; however, the size and scope of the problem must be determined prior to exploring desires to change.

## USING QUESTIONS IN THE MID-STAGES OF THE BUYING JOURNEY: ASSESSING SOLUTION DEFINITION

Once buyers have moved beyond the identify needs stage of their journey, they have typically decided that their problems are big and thorny enough to fix. Their thinking shifts from "How bad is it?" to "How do I fix it?" They go from thinking about the downsides of their current situation to thinking about how they'd like to improve it. They ask questions like, "What is most important to me in a solution? What is less important? What trade-offs am I prepared to make?" The buyers' thinking becomes more aspirational. They begin to establish criteria they will use to evaluate solutions. These criteria—or requirements—are very important in narrowing down the field of possible solutions.

Because buyers shift from focusing on problems to focusing on solutions in the mid-stages, agile salespeople adjust their approach to align to this shift. The best-case scenario for a salesperson is to get involved early in the buyers' journey and shape how the buyers view their problems, as well as how the buyers define which criteria are most important to them in making a change.

Shaping the buyers' criteria is an important component of being able to effectively differentiate the seller's solutions against competing alternatives. It sets the salesperson up for success because competitive solutions will be evaluated through the lens of the criteria the salesperson helped shape. Any salesperson who has participated in a request for proposal (RFP) for which they had little fore knowledge has felt the pain of this predicament. It is rare to win a deal that someone else—namely, your competitor—has helped shape.

**It is rare to win a deal that someone else—namely your competitor—has helped shape.**

In the mid-stages of the buyers' journey, when buyers are focusing on what they want and why they want it, it is most effective for salespeople to use a gain-driven approach to questioning as indicated in Figure 4.6. Sellers need to understand what the buyers want, why they want it, what is most and least important, and how the buyers will determine fit. They need to establish the criteria the buyer will use to evaluate alternatives. It is like the conversation you might have with a real estate agent when you are looking for a house. The real estate agent will ask you a series of questions about what you want in a house. How big? What area? How many bedrooms and bathrooms do you want? Is a yard important? How about a garage? On and on it goes. This establishment of criteria is necessary to narrow the field. Otherwise, the options are over-whelming. The same is true of your buyers.

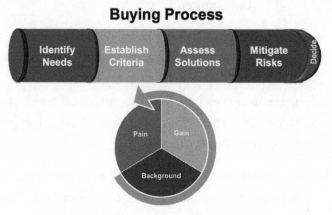

FIGURE 4.6 **Using a Gain-Driven Approach**
*Source:* VantagePoint Performance.

This shift in salesperson behavior—from using a pain-driven approach early in the buying journey to using a gain-driven approach in the mid-stages of the buying journey—is a hallmark of agile salespeople. Most consultative selling methodologies miss this important distinction of using questions differently depending on the stage (early, mid, or late) in the buyers' journey. The example below highlights how a salesperson might use questions differently in the scenarios shared earlier in this chapter. In scenario 1, the logistics manager is in the mid-stages of their buying journey and interested in discussing and assessing solutions. The buyer has already explored the size and scope of the noise issues and is now actively looking for ways to reduce noise.

## Sample Gain-Driven Approach

*Background question:* Can you tell me what prompted your call to Quiet-Tech?

*Gain questions:* What types of noise reduction solutions have you considered? Are there specific types of products you've researched to address your concerns? Can you tell me more about what seems appropriate?

*Gain questions:* When you spoke about reducing the noise in your administrative area, you mentioned that avoiding a major construction project is important. What other requirements do you have in solving this problem? Is time to completion important? How about minimizing disruption during the installation process?

As you can see, these questions are primarily gain driven, designed to better understand what the logistics manager hopes to accomplish and which requirements and criteria are most important. This is an example of using a gain-driven approach to meet the logistics manager at the appropriate point in their buying journey.

This awareness and the ability to shift between a pain-driven and gain-driven approach are necessary to establish a foundation for agility and equip sellers to flex their approach across the buyers' journey. We now move to the late stages of the buyers' journey and use questions to assess buyers' perceived risks and concerns.

## USING QUESTIONS IN THE LATE STAGES OF THE BUYING JOURNEY: MITIGATING RISK

The late stages of the buyer's journey include another shift in the buyers' objectives and motivators. Recall that early in the buying journey, buyers are asking the question, "Do I need to change?" They are evaluating the size and scope of their problems to determine if they are big enough to fix. Midway through the buying journey, once buyers have decided change is warranted, they shift their attention to what they want to achieve by making a change.

Motivation is very aspirational, focused on buyers' wants, buying criteria, and clarifying the ideal solution. As buyers narrow down the scope of potential solutions to a vital few, their objectives shift yet again and become focused on the potential risks and downsides of making the change. A mix of background, pain, and gain questions are also relevant in these late stages.

Typically, the sellers who make it to the very late stages of an opportunity have been involved in earlier stages; however, it is not uncommon in today's buying environment for buyers to do significant research prior to contacting a salesperson. In those cases, sellers become involved when the buyers are actively evaluating solutions and have identified a short list of potential providers. Once the short list has been determined, buyers look under every rock, dot every *I*, and cross every *T*. They do their due diligence and look for ways to minimize risk and pave the way for a smooth implementation.

During these late stages, buyers may be less responsive, taking far longer to respond to salespeople than during earlier stages. They do this because they are doing their due diligence and need time to sort it all out. This reduction in communication is often seen by salespeople as "radio silence." It is uncomfortable and feels very ambiguous to salespeople. The biggest mistake many salespeople make in this situation is to amp up their communication while the buyers reduce theirs. In other words, when the buyers become radio silent, salespeople often become radioactive. This behavior is counterproductive and often irritates buyers.

The best salespeople anticipate this shift, are prepared to address it proactively, and shift their behavior to a more empathetic, understanding approach. A conversation in the late stages between a buyer and seller may sound something like this:

*Seller:* Hello John, thanks for taking the meeting. I've noticed a drop-off in our communication, and typically when that happens, there is a concern that needs to be addressed. Are you having any worries about the potential implementation? Are there specific concerns that you would like to address to increase your confidence in your decision?

*Buyer:* Well, now that you mention it, I have been worried about disruption to the administrative staff, even though you assured me that wouldn't happen.

*Seller:* I can understand your concern. You want to respect the productivity of your employees and minimize disruption to whatever degree possible. When other customers of mine have had this concern, one way we were able to help them resolve it was by speaking to existing customers who had the same concerns, went forward with the implementation, and experienced minimal disruption. Would that be something you feel would help?

*Buyer:* Yes, I would like to speak to someone in a similar situation if possible. Maybe someone with a similar plant configuration.

*Seller:* I can arrange a conversation.

In the above example, the salesperson acknowledged the shift in communication. Then the salesperson provided context about when this has happened in the past and in what circumstances. The seller then used pain questions to determine if any concerns existed. Once the concern about disruption surfaced, the seller then acknowledged the concern and made reflective statements to display empathy. The seller then used a gain question to determine if the buyer was open to the suggestion.

In the late stages, it is imperative that the salesperson look to minimize possible pain rather than amplify it. Again, this is how agile sellers shift their own behavior to adjust to early-, mid-, and late-stage conversations.

## SUMMARY

This first part of our decision-making framework for foundational sales agility focused on using questions to assess the buyers' position within their buying journey, the level of problem awareness, the buyers' definition of their desired solution, and any perceived risks the buyers were feeling about moving forward. We mentioned that agile sellers adjust their sales approach according to the buyers' location within their buying journey.

The next important step agile sellers take is to plan each interaction so that this alignment is apparent to the buyers and it is relevant to helping the buyers move seamlessly across their buying journey. In the next chapter, we offer guidance for how to choose and plan the best path and effectively execute sales conversations differently at different points along the buyers' journey.

## KEY TAKEAWAYS

- Effective consultative selling must be grounded in the buying journey, reflecting different sales objectives and tactics reflective of the buyers' position within their buying journey.

- Assessing the buyers' location within their buying journey is the first and most important factor to consider when attempting to determine the best sales approach.

- Agile sellers use a combination of background, pain, and gain questions to understand and influence buyer behavior.

- Pain questions are particularly important during the early stages of the buyers' journey, building urgency and a case for change. Pain questions help us gauge the level of the buyers' problem awareness.

- Gain questions are vital in the mid-stages of the buyers' journey, helping the seller shape and influence buyer needs and buying criteria. Gain questions help us uncover buyer needs and shape buying criteria to help influence the buyers' solution definition.

- Selling efforts late in the buyers' journey involve helping the buyers reduce perceived risk and increase confidence in making a high-quality, low-risk buying decision.

## CHAPTER 5

# Choosing, Planning, and Executing Sales Conversations Across the Buying Journey

In the last chapter we explored in detail how agile salespeople assess the buying situation. We examined how agile sellers use questions to assess the buyers' location in the buying journey, the level of problem awareness, the buyers' definition of their desired solution, as well as perceived risks.

In this chapter we take a deep dive into how agile sellers choose the best path and plan for their choice, and then how agile sellers execute calls differently at different points along the buying journey.

## CHOOSING AND PLANNING FOR FOUNDATIONAL SALES AGILITY ACROSS THE BUYING JOURNEY

In this section, we begin by exploring the anatomy of a sales conversation. You have most likely been exposed to this type of content many times over your sales career. However, we introduce this framework for sales conversations only to provide the appropriate context for planning interactions differently at different stages of the buyers' journey. If the goal of foundational sales agility is to align our sales approach to the buyer, we need to know how to adjust our conversations to reflect that alignment.

In Figure 5.1, we see the decision-making framework for foundational agility, including this second step: choosing for agility.

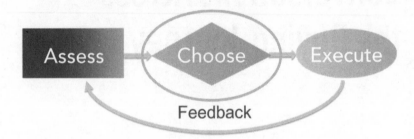

FIGURE 5.1 **Choosing and Planning for Foundational Agility**
*Source:* VantagePoint Performance.

Navigating a sales conversation with prospects and customers is one of the first things sellers must master to perfect their craft. Effective sales conversations are not random. They follow a predictable sequence. Just as buyers follow a process, sellers do too.

To plan effectively for a sales conversation, we need a path to follow and some ground rules for how to engage with buyers in a collaborative and effective way. We will dig into the specifics of how to navigate a sales call, and once we've established a baseline, we will then examine how to plan sales calls differently at different points along the buyers' journey.

Figure 5.2 represents the flow of a collaborative sales conversation. The degree to which a seller effectively executes this flow determines the impact of the conversation. Every salesperson knows that the quality of planning has a dramatic impact on the quality of sales execution. To that end, we will briefly unpack each step of the sales conversation, how to do it, and why it is necessary.

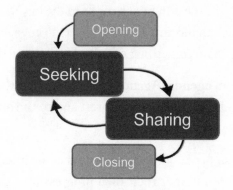

FIGURE 5.2 **The Flow of a Collaborative Sales Conversation**
*Source:* VantagePoint Performance.

Once we've established this baseline, we will examine how agile sellers incorporate buyer psychology and an understanding of the buying journey to plan and adapt sales behavior across the early, mid, and late stages of the buying journey. We will build upon this baseline understanding to investigate how to plan differently at different buying stages.

## The Opening

The most effective sales calls start with a good opening. The opening lays the groundwork for a productive conversation between buyers and sellers. It represents a path forward that both buyers and sellers can agree upon. There are four things sellers need to do during their opening:

1. Establish **rapport**. Create a connection with the buyers that builds an environment of trust.

2. State the **reason** for the meeting. This answers the question, "Why are we meeting today?" This reason must be important to the buyers.

3. Highlight the potential **benefit** to the buyers. This provides an incentive for the buyers to engage in dialogue, giving them something of value for the time spent.

4. Share an **agenda**. Agendas set the table for the flow of the call and give the buyers comfort and confidence that their time will be well spent.

While these steps may seem obvious, they are often overlooked. Salespeople often hinder their own progress by either spending too much time chatting and building rapport or launching into dialogue without setting the proper context. A good opening paves the way for a productive, satisfying conversation.

## Seeking and Giving Information

As you see in Figure 5.2, there is an interplay between seeking and giving information. This is an important point. In many training programs, we learned to ask all our discovery questions prior to offering any information to the buyers. This doesn't work in our personal lives, and it doesn't work in sales. Many questioning methods are complex and overengineered. They assume that buyers have all the time in the world and have nothing better to do than answer our questions.

In today's chaotic, overinformed buying environment, this couldn't be further from the truth. Buyers want a compelling and interesting conversation, not an interrogation followed by a data dump. The most effective sellers seek information about the buyers' situation, their problems, and their needs in a collaborative way.

Salespeople must provide information to the buyers, but what type of information should they provide, and when? Most sellers think that giving information in a sales call is about providing details of their solutions and how those solutions meet buyer needs. Most of us learn how to tie solution features with benefits to the buyers. This feature-benefit linkage is important, but it is only part of the story. What information we share and when we share it is also tied to foundational agility. The most effective sellers share the right types of information at the right time aligned to the buyers' situation.

As you will recall, we use background questions to tease out the specifics of the buyers' situation, pain questions to uncover and clarify the buyers' problems, and gain questions to explore the buyers' needs and desires (Figure 5.3). We assume that if you are reading this, you've had exposure to many different questioning approaches in the past. Our goal here is to help you learn how to flex your approach based on the situation you face, regardless of the specific questioning model you use. More later in this chapter on how to share information effectively.

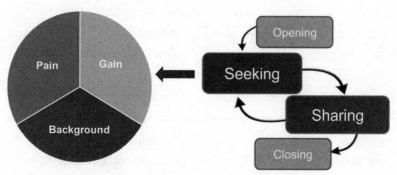

FIGURE 5.3 **Seeking Information with Questions**
*Source:* VantagePoint Performance.

## Gaining Incremental Commitment

Effective sales conversations lead to actionable next steps. This is not a surprise, but sadly it is also not a common practice. High-performing salespeople always have a goal in mind. In fact, they have more than one positive outcome in mind. If they don't get the next step they want, they have a few alternatives to fall back on. Figure 5.4 shows a ladder of commitment from good to better to best.

FIGURE 5.4 **Commitment Ladder**
*Source:* VantagePoint Performance.

This intentional planning for actionable next steps is a key behavior of high-performing sellers. In fact, our research indicated that gaining incremental commitments along the buying journey is the consultative tactic most highly correlated to performance. These incremental commitments dramatically improve the likelihood of gaining the final purchase commitment from the buyer.

Figure 5.5 shows the relative influence of three consultative tactics on wins. As you can see, obtaining commitment is by far the most influential tactic. This surprised us, but not after we examined the findings more thoroughly. If salespeople can make consistent, measurable progress as they navigate an opportunity, they are much more likely to win. To that end, the most effective way to plan a sales call is to begin with the end in mind. If we start with our destination in mind, we have a much better chance of mapping out the best route to get there.

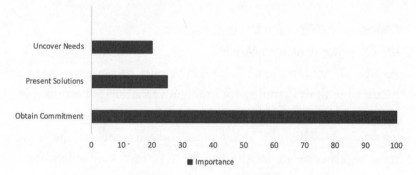

FIGURE 5.5 **Influence of Consultative Tactics on Wins**
*Source:* VantagePoint Performance.

Now that we've detailed how high-performing sellers navigate sales conversations, it's time to turn our attention to how they navigate them differently based on the buying situation they face. This is where we marry buyer behavior and seller behavior to equip salespeople with the foundation for sales agility.

## Planning Sales Calls Across the Buying Journey

We've clarified the most effective way to navigate sales conversations and ensure appropriate collaboration. Now we must take into consideration how we adjust and adapt those sales conversations to align to the buyers' position within their buying journey. This is the part that many consultative sales methodologies miss.

The idea that we can conduct our sales calls the same way regardless of the buyers' situation is like thinking a quarterback can keep running the same play throughout a football game and win. It doesn't make sense. Just as the quarterback must consider the defensive situation prior to calling a play, the best salespeople consider the buyers' position within their buying journey prior to running their next sales play. The most agile sellers align their sales behavior to the buyers, not the other way around.

### Choosing and Planning Conversations at the Early Stage: Identify Needs

As we indicated in Figure 5.2, effective sales conversations have a predictable flow. Planning for sales conversations is best done in reverse, focusing on closing and working back through the conversation flow. Because incremental commitments are the tactic most highly correlated with wins, the most successful sellers begin with the end in mind. See Figure 5.6 for a depiction of this reverse engineering.

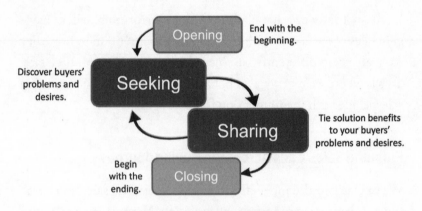

FIGURE 5.6  **Call Planning Best Practices**
*Source:* VantagePoint Performance.

When we plan this way, the entire plan hangs together much better and increases the likelihood that we will conduct the conversation in a way that leads to the outcome we want. This is the way you plan other things in your life as well. If you were to plan a vacation, one of your first decisions would be the destination and then other decisions would support that focus.

We will continue to use the same two scenarios from Chapter 4. This will give us a concrete way to examine how to choose and plan differently for an early-stage conversation versus a mid-stage conversation. In scenario 2 (below), we concluded that the plant manager was very early in her buying journey, and she is willing to speak to us; however, there is no indication that problems exist. The only reason the plant manager is interested in speaking with us is due to her recent conversation with her friend, the logistics manager. We will use call planning best practices: beginning with the end in mind and identifying our good, better, and best outcome:

> *Scenario 2:* The buyer is a plant manager at a medical manufacturing plant. She attended a conference last week on advances in manufacturing practices and ran into her old friend the logistics manager. They caught up on recent events, and they even chatted about the noise problem the logistics manager recently addressed.
>
> This piqued the plant manager's interest to learn more about whether some of the same issues were afoot within her own plant. Employee productivity is very important in all manufacturing plants, and hers was no exception. The logistics manager passed on the name and contact information of the plant manager to the QuietTech salesperson. The salesperson reached out and scheduled a conversation with the plant manager for the following week.

### Commitment Ladder of Incremental Outcomes

*Good:* A follow-up meeting with the plant manager to tour the plant

*Better:* A meeting with the supervisors and administrative staff to explore the noise situation

*Best:* A commitment to a noise study that would involve the supervisors, line personnel, and administrative staff

## Sharing Information

Since this is an early-stage conversation, the plant manager is not likely to be interested in discussing solutions. If the seller is to share relevant information, it may be in the form of stories or examples of how QuietTech has analyzed noise levels in other plants, the process for doing an analysis, and/or possibly scenarios involving other QuietTech customers in the same industry as the plant manager.

## Seeking Information

Early-stage conversations are designed to examine the buyer's level of problem awareness. To that end, the salesperson must be ready to explore the likely problems the plant manager is experiencing, as well as the size and scope of those problems (Table 5.1). It is useful to consider the potential noise problems and their likely consequences. It may be useful to map out the problems and consequences in the buyer's terms. This provides the fodder for powerful pain questions the seller can ask.

#### TABLE 5.1 EXAMPLES OF POTENTIAL PROBLEMS

| Potential Problems | Likely Consequences |
|---|---|
| • Excess noise in the offices surrounding the assembly line | • Irritated employees, looking for alternative places to work and meet |
| • Problems focusing on administrative work | • Missed deadlines<br>• Excessive complaints |

In order for these problems to be relevant, the salesperson needs to understand the layout of the plant. This can be accomplished through a few targeted background questions:

## Background Questions

- What is the proximity of the administrative staff to the plant floor?

- What hours does the line operate, and to what degree does that overlap with the daytime administrative hours?

## Pain Questions

- Have you had complaints of excessive noise in the plant? Who has complained, and what were the details of their complaints?

- How often have people complained about their ability to focus due to excessive noise?

- Have there been instances in which employees had to roam around and find alternative places to work?

- How about productivity? How often are deadlines missed because of noise-related work interruptions?

It is much easier to develop powerful pain questions if you've anticipated the likely problems and consequences the buyers are experiencing. Again, it is this intentional focus, beginning with the outcome in mind and planning backward, that leads to the most powerful sales conversations. Once you've mapped out the desired commitments, the potential information you can share, and the questions you'd like to ask, it is time to develop an opening.

---

It is much easier to develop powerful pain questions if you've anticipated the likely problems and consequences the buyers are experiencing.

---

## Developing the Opening

The reason the opening is planned last is because once everything else has been mapped out, developing an effective opening is easy. You have full context to pull from when considering the best way to open the conversation:

> *Reason:* To get a better understanding of the plant and the associated noise levels.

> *Benefit:* This will allow QuietTech to understand how noise affects the plant operations and make recommendations to improve the flow of work.

> *Agenda:* Explore the current situation on the plant floor, determine which issues, if any, exist, and explore the appropriate steps needed to address identified issues.

This simple, yet powerful method of planning ensures a purposeful approach to buyer-seller interactions. It lets buyers know that the salesperson values their time and is prepared to use it wisely. It also ensures that the conversation that ensues is relevant to the buyers' location in their buying journey. The examples we've been using are purposely simplistic so that we don't overcomplicate the process. This same process for planning a sales conversation works with simple and highly complex sales.

### Choosing and Planning Conversations at the Mid-Stages: Establish Criteria and Assess Solutions

Planning shifts as the buying journey progresses. We will continue to use our scenarios from Chapter 4. In this instance, we will use scenario 1 (below). We concluded that the logistics manager in scenario 1 was in the assess solutions stage and actively looking for noise reduction solutions. We know that because the logistics manager reached out to QuietTech to explore noise reduction solutions. This proactive request on the part of the buyer is a sure indication that the buyer is actively evaluating solutions:

> *Scenario 1:* The buyer is a logistics manager within a manufacturing plant. The plant supervisors have received a variety of noise complaints from the workers in the offices surrounding the production line. Apparently, the noise levels are distracting and impeding productivity of the administrative staff.
>
> The plant manager has explored this issue and feels that the noise complaints are valid. The plant manager has tasked the logistics manager with finding a solution to reduce noise in the administrative area.
>
> The logistics manager has researched noise-reducing options online, found a few potential solutions that wouldn't require a significant construction project, and identified a few companies that offer these low-disruption solutions. The logistics manager has secured a meeting with a salesperson from QuietTech, one of the potential vendors.

As we indicated in earlier chapters, buyers have different objectives and motivators as they progress through their buying journey. Once buyers have decided they have a problem big enough to fix, they shift their attention to what they want, rather than what they currently have. The buyers' thinking and associated behavior become aspirational, focused on what they want moving forward. Our plan must reflect this type of buyer thinking and align salesperson behavior accordingly.

This conversation will be more gain driven due to the buyer's position in their buying journey. Let's piece together a relevant plan for the conversation based on our call planning best practices. We will begin with the end in mind:

### Commitment Ladder of Incremental Outcomes

*Good:* A referral conversation with a satisfied QuietTech customer

*Better:* A plant visit to a satisfied QuietTech customer location

*Best:* A trial period for portable noise reduction products on the plant floor

### Sharing Information

Since this is a mid-stage conversation, the logistics manager will be keenly interested in discussing noise reduction solutions. If the seller is to share relevant information, it may be in the form of stories or examples of how QuietTech has addressed and reduced noise levels in other plants.

The specific types of solutions implemented, the positive outcomes of those solutions, and the improvements in employee satisfaction and productivity can be shared.

### Seeking Information

Mid-stage conversations are designed to examine the buyers' vision of a desired solution. To that end, the salesperson must be ready to explore the buyers' desires as well as any details or specific requirements regarding a desired solution. It is useful to map out the potential needs and desires the buyers are likely to have, as well as the specific improvements, and the potential payoffs they seek, in the buyers' terms (Table 5.2).

Thinking this through from the buyers' perspective is critical to avoiding the temptation to use your solution as a lens. Remember, people like to buy but not to be sold. Considering the buyers' desires and payoffs will provide the fodder for powerful gain questions.

TABLE 5.2 **EXAMPLES OF POTENTIAL NEEDS AND DESIRES**

| Potential Needs and Desires | Likely Payoff |
|---|---|
| • Increase separation between the plant floor and the administrative offices | • Reduced noise distractions <br> • Improved working conditions |
| • Minimal construction or disruption to current workflow | • Maintain plant operations and employee productivity during implementation |

Although these are the most typical needs and desires articulated by buyers in this situation, the salesperson needs some context to determine what steps have already been taken to address the noise issues. Otherwise, the salesperson will have an incomplete picture of the buyers' process and progress in their buying journey. This can be determined through a few targeted background questions:

### Background Questions

- What have you learned thus far in the research you've done about noise reduction solutions?

- Are you evaluating any other suppliers?

- Have you tried other noise-reducing options in the past?

- What is your desired timeline for implementing a noise reduction solution in the plant?

### Gain Questions

- What are some of the primary requirements you have for noise reduction on the plant floor?

- To what degree does that involve an improved separation between the administrative offices and the plant floor?

- Are you hoping that by reducing noise distractions, you can improve employee satisfaction? How about morale?

- How important is it for you to avoid disruption to the current workflow while implementing the noise reduction solution?

- Will a low-construction solution help you achieve a smoother transition? How so?

It is much easier to develop powerful gain questions if you've anticipated the likely desires and potential payoff the buyer is hoping to experience. As before in our planning efforts, we develop the opening last:

**Developing the Opening**

*Reason:* To get a better understanding of desires and specific requirements the buyer has for reducing noise in the plant.

*Benefit:* This will increase your confidence that you will select the best, most relevant solution to improve conditions in the plant.

*Agenda:* Explore the steps the buyer has taken to this point, which requirements have surfaced, and the implications of those requirements for solving the current noise problems.

At this point, we've examined how to assess the buyers' location in the buying journey, their level of problem awareness, and the buyers' solution definition. We've given details of how to plan differently at the early and mid-stages of the buying journey, when the biggest shifts in buyer motivators occur. Although we alluded to different aspects of sales execution, this next section explores the goals and potential pitfalls of aligning seller behavior to the buying journey and executing sales conversations effectively.

## EXECUTING SALES CALLS FOR FOUNDATIONAL SALES AGILITY ACROSS THE BUYING JOURNEY

Figure 5.7 reflects the last step of our decision-making framework for foundational sales agility. There is a constant interplay between assessing, choosing, planning, and executing conversations as buyers navigate their buying journey. Most consultative sales training programs and methodologies focus on sales execution. They have a variety of practice opportunities to plan and execute different consultative sales tactics. The lion's share of our guidance in this chapter is on assessing the buying situation. This overemphasis on buyer assessment is a hallmark of agile sellers, as well as agile individuals in other domains such as sports, the military, and first responders. The better, more accurate the assessment, the higher the likelihood that execution will be relevant and effective.

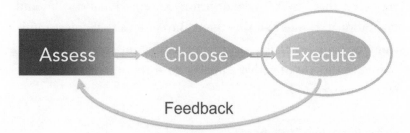

FIGURE 5.7 **Foundational Agility in Action**
*Source:* VantagePoint Performance.

We will explore the finer points of executing sales conversations early and midway through the buyer's journey, paying particular attention to potential trouble spots and failure points along the way. We omit executing sales calls at the late stages of the buyer's journey because we addressed most of the necessary information in the planning section of this chapter.

## Executing Sales Conversations Early in the Buying Journey

One aspect of execution that warrants further discussion here is the interpersonal nuances of conducting sales conversations at different points along the buying journey. Early-stage conversations differ from mid- or late-stage conversations.

One of the biggest challenges to effective dialogue is to get the buyer talking. To that end, we've offered background, pain, and gain questions to uncover buyer problems, determine the severity of those problems, and then develop them into buyer needs and desires. Many sellers are uncomfortable using this pain-driven approach to questioning. Some feel it may be perceived as intrusive to the buyer.

This represents a challenge for salespeople because research is very clear that buyers make decisions for emotional reasons and find rational reasons to justify them. Buyers are also far more motivated by pain, particularly early in their buying journey. We recommend the use of active empathy to soften the hard edges of pain-driven conversations.

### Using Reflective Statements

*Reflective statements* are statements that acknowledge the buyer's words, ideas, problems, and needs. It is a form of clarification and empathetic listening. The use of reflective statements shows the buyer that the seller is listening and makes the conversation more collaborative. We will use our previous examples to make this point more salient. The following example is based on scenario 1 (the logistics manager):

*Seller:* Have you had complaints of excessive noise in the plant? Who has complained, and what were the details of their complaints?

*Buyer:* Yes, we've had a lot of complaints. It is primarily the staff whose offices are closest to the production floor.

*Seller:* How often have people complained about their ability to focus being disrupted due to excessive noise?

*Buyer:* It is a constant problem. People must look for alternative places to do their work. This takes time and distracts them from their tasks.

*Seller:* I can imagine that is very frustrating. People typically don't like to waste time, especially when it feels unnecessary.

*Buyer:* Yes, people feel that we are making their jobs harder than they need to be.

The seller's last statement is an example of a reflective statement that shows active empathy by acknowledging the buyer's possible frustrations. It is a way of relating to the buyer and the buyer's situation. These reflective statements can be used at multiple points during the conversation to keep it from sounding like an interrogation. Reflective statements also ensure that the seller is listening actively and not making assumptions.

### Giving Information While Maintaining Curiosity

The interplay of seeking and giving information is the secret to effective sales conversations. Salespeople must resist the impulse to jump in too quickly with solutions, but they must also share solutions in a way that engages the buyer. One of the nuances of the most agile salespeople is that they share just enough information to pique the buyer's interest without overdoing it. The best example we can share about the importance of maintaining curiosity is comparing the sales conversation to a first date.

---

**One of the nuances of the most agile salespeople is that they share just enough information to pique the buyer's interest without overdoing it.**

---

Imagine if on your first date, the other person spent the entire time telling you all about themselves. This can be overwhelming, and it is not likely to lead to a second date. We all want give-and-take in our conversations. Buyers are no different. The example below uses gain questions to maintain buyer interest while discussing solutions:

*Seller:* It sounds like reducing the noise for your administrative staff is very important. Is this something you hope to address quickly?

*Buyer:* Yes, I'd like to see something in place in the next 60 days.

*Seller:* Yes, it is not uncommon for these types of projects to be very urgent. We've worked with other clients to deploy our low-construction noise solutions quickly. . . . Would a timeline that completed the work in the next 45 days be desirable?

*Buyer:* Yes, that's faster than I anticipated.

*Seller:* Excellent. How excited will you be to eliminate all the noise complaints?

*Buyer:* Whew, that will be a relief!

The way the seller is interacting with the buyer is highly collaborative. The seller has not clearly detailed how they will deploy their solution in 45 days. Those details will come later. Meanwhile, the buyer feels good that the seller can meet their 60-day installation requirement but hasn't been immediately bogged down with too much detail. The seller provided just enough information to satisfy the buyer without inundating them. The seller also reengaged the buyer with the last question, "How excited will you be to eliminate all the noise complaints?" This is an example of using a gain question to keep the conversation collaborative and test the buyer's interest.

The give-and-take, as well as the small reveal of solution information, keeps buyers curious to learn more. Psychologically speaking, maintaining interest is vital to a powerful sales call. Curiosity keeps us engaged in conversations. If you think about curiosity in your own life, how many times have you watched a bad movie all the way to the end because you want to see what happens? We want our curiosity satisfied, even if we are not fully committed to a situation or an outcome.

## Executing Sales Conversations in the Mid-Stages of the Buying Journey

When buyers have moved beyond the early stages of their journey, this indicates that they are open to change and are motivated to explore solutions. The salespeople must adapt their behavior accordingly. As we mentioned earlier, these mid-stage sales conversations are primarily gain driven. The same points we made about being collaborative and maintaining curiosity remain important, but there are a few other nuances of conducting mid-stage sales conversations that warrant further examination.

One of the important nuances is the distinction between buyer needs and the criteria buyers will use to evaluate alternative solutions. The most successful sellers are very intentional about how they shape buyer needs into buying criteria. This shaping of buying criteria goes a long way to setting sellers up for effective differentiation when offering solutions.

### Shaping Needs and Desires into Buying Criteria

The difference between needs and desires and buying criteria is the level of specificity. The examples in Table 5.3 are taken from scenario 1 discussed earlier.

TABLE 5.3 **EXAMPLES OF NEEDS AND DESIRES VERSUS BUYING CRITERIA**

| Needs and Desires | Buying Criteria |
|---|---|
| Increase separation between the plant floor and the administrative offices | I want a portable barrier between the administrative offices and the plant floor that reduces noise by 75 percent over current levels. |
| Minimal construction or disruption to current workflow | I want a solution that can be installed during working hours, has no impact on the configuration of the line, and won't shut the line down. |

You'll notice that the statements on the left are gain oriented, but they are not highly specific. It is the job of the salesperson to move the client from vague needs to specific buying criteria. It is especially powerful when the seller can shape these buying criteria in ways that favor the seller's solution.

Let's examine our first example above as a conversation between the buyer and seller. In this case, the seller's solution reduces noise better than competing alternatives. Competing low-construction portable solutions reduce noise by about 50 percent. This is a strong differentiator for the QuietTech salesperson, and it should be leveraged. The conversation might unfold like the one below:

*Seller:* How important is it for you to establish separation between the administrative offices and the plant floor?

*Buyer:* Very important. That's why we're exploring solutions right now. This problem needs to be resolved.

*Seller:* I understand. I realize you're frustrated by the complaints. When you say separation between the offices and the plant floor, are you hoping to dramatically reduce the current noise levels by up to 75 percent? Would that accomplish your goal?

*Buyer:* Yes, absolutely. If we could reduce noise levels by up to 75 percent, people could work without being distracted.

*Seller:* So, just to clarify, you'd like a significant noise reduction over current levels—and reducing the noise by 75 percent would meet that requirement.

*Buyer:* Yes, that's right.

*Seller:* Does that mean that any noise reduction solution that reduced noise by only 50 percent would be insufficient?

*Buyer:* Yes. A 50 percent reduction would not be sufficient to address the noise concerns. I would prefer a 75 percent reduction to be safe.

In this case, the seller very skillfully set the requirement at 75 percent. The seller even confirmed that a 50 percent reduction in noise would be insufficient. If this buyer meets with other noise reduction companies, you can bet he will be asking about levels of noise reduction and comparing them to QuietTech. In this instance, the seller might go even further and explore how other solutions that reduce noise by only 50 percent might be inadequate. This would differentiate the QuietTech solution while planting seeds of doubt in the buyer's mind about competing solutions. This nuance of using gain questions to shape needs and desires into buying criteria is a best practice of high-performing, agile sales-people.

> This nuance of using gain questions to shape needs
> and desires into buying criteria is a best practice
> of high-performing, agile salespeople.

## SUMMARY

We've examined how the most agile sellers deploy founda-tional agility by planning and executing sales conversations differently at different points along the buyers' journey. This deep understanding of the core elements of foundational agility sets sell-ers up for taking the next important step, embracing and deploying situational agility.

In our next chapters, we unpack the vital components of situa-tional agility.

## KEY TAKEAWAYS

- Effective sales conversations follow a predicable flow:
  - An opening that sets the tone and establishes desired outcomes for the conversation
  - Seeking information about the buyer and the buying situation
  - Sharing information relevant to the buyers' location within their buying journey
  - Closing for an actionable next step in the buyers' journey

- The content of each step varies depending upon the buyers' location within their buying journey.

- Planning for sales calls early in the buyers' journey involves discovery of the buyers' pain points and overall consequences of their current state, as well as desires for a future state.

- Planning for sales calls midway through the buyers' journey involves understanding buyer needs and specific buying criteria buyers will use to make their buying decision, as well as how well competing alternatives fit their buying criteria.

- Planning for sales calls late in the buyers' journey involves understanding the buyers' perceived risks and concerns and finding the most effective means to mitigate their risks.

- All planning efforts for sales conversations should begin with the desired outcome in mind and work backward to develop a targeted plan.

# PART III

# THE PILLARS OF
# SALES AGILITY

## CHAPTER 6

# Situational Agility and the Components of the Agility Enablement System

Let's begin by clarifying that situational agility is not the same thing as spontaneity. They are very different things. The online dictionary *Oxford Languages* defines *spontaneity* as "proceeding from natural feeling without external constraint" and "arising from a momentary impulse." Spontaneity does not account for opportunity cost—that is, what you may be giving up by making your *conscious choice*. It does not require any preparation or planning or require any retrospection after the fact. It is immediate, reactive, and "directed internally."

In contrast, *situational agility* requires preparation and forethought, as well as an acute observation of the present. Situational agility requires a mindset and skill set that take focus and effort to perfect. Spontaneity and situational agility can be hard to distinguish in the heat of the moment. If you have ever wondered why some people respond to situations more effectively than others, you have likely wrestled with this distinction. Differences in responses can seem random, but they seldom are. There is usually more to the story.

## THE OODA LOOP

John Boyd, arguably one of the most successful fighter pilots in history, wondered about this during his career as a US Air Force fighter pilot.[1] Because of Boyd's approach and dramatic success in enemy engagement, he was asked to create a framework that had wide-ranging implications in the military, legal profession, gaming industry, and now sales. He is seen as one of the most influential strategists of the twentieth century, and he helped articulate how agile decision-making happens.

John Boyd wondered why some pilots were more effective in combat than others. Why some appeared to know how to anticipate and avoid enemy fire while others could not. After all, they received the same training, and they had the same equipment. In searching for the answer to this question, he became one of the first to articulate how and why agility was essential to success as a fighter pilot.[2]

Boyd believed that the key to victory, in battle and in business, was the ability to create situations in which one could make appropriate decisions more quickly than one's opponent.[3] Let's break that statement down a bit because there are some critical concepts here. First, "the ability to create situations" indicates that this is not a passive process. Agility is possible only when a person has put some effort into understanding or even creating the situation. Second, "one can make appropriate decisions quickly," or make decisions that fit the situation. This destroys the misconception that there is one right way—there are potentially many ways to behave based upon the circumstances you encounter.

Boyd believed that the key to victory, in battle and in business, was the ability to create situations in which one could make appropriate decisions more quickly than one's opponent.

Boyd further hypothesized that we, meaning individuals or organizations, are in a continuous cycle of interaction with our environment. Boyd used the term "OODA loop" to describe this relationship (Figure 6.1).

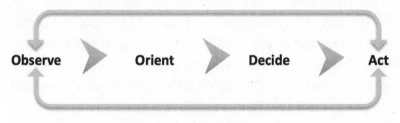

FIGURE 6.1 **The OODA Loop**
*Source:* Inspired by OODA loop images at OpexSociety.org.

- *Observe:* Gather information from the environment.

- *Orient:* Use your perspective, your mental frame, to make sense of the information gathered.

- *Decide:* Choose a course of action that reflects your perspective—how you made sense of the observed data.

- *Act:* Execute the decision.

These four actions happen in a continual cycle—hence the name OODA loop—and they can overlap. For example, imagine that while in the process of deciding a course of action, you become aware of a new piece of information (observation), so before you act, you double back to orienting and verify that your decision still makes sense. The OODA loop made agility tangible for fighter pilots and helped pave the way to make it teachable as well.

## CAREERS BASED ON AGILITY

If you want to see agility in action, visit any hospital emergency room. Go for a ride with a firefighting crew, or spend some time with professional athletic teams. If you want to understand how each of those groups teaches agility, spend a lot of time with them and ask questions. That is exactly what a team led by Dr. Leff Bonney of the Florida State University's Sales Institute did.

Recall that Dr. Bonney and his team led a series of studies that showed that higher-performing salespeople consistently demonstrated the ability to flex their approach based on the customers' buying situation (see Chapter 2). Many believed (and some still do) that agility is a personality trait, an innate ability that cannot be taught. Yet, if this was true, how did the types of aforementioned organizations take ordinary people and teach them to do the extraordinary? Agility may or may not be a trait some are born with; however, that does not prevent it from being something that the rest of us can learn.

Dr. Bonney's hypothesis was straightforward: if he could understand what these diverse organizations did to teach agility, he could use those same principles to teach agility to sales professionals, enabling all salespeople to emulate the highest performers. In working closely with organizations that had mastered the training of agility, he witnessed the OODA loop in action.

Emergency room staff must do several things quickly and well. First, they must use their senses to observe and take note of what is happening around them. Next, they must **o**rient, or make sense of the information they have gathered, paying attention to the most pertinent information. Then, they must choose (**d**ecide) the most effective course of action based on their training and experience. Finally, they must execute (**a**ct) on that course of action well. They must do this very quickly and confidently.

The same applies to firefighters. When responding to a fire, firefighters walk into an unknown situation and begin by observing: What do they see? What can they smell? What can they feel? They use that information, combined with their training and experience, to orient—that is, determine what is likely happening. Based on their quick assessment, they decide what to do and execute on that plan. For example, the way smoke moves is an important source of intelligence for firefighters. If they misread or ignore that information, the consequences can be fatal. If smoke is leaving a building in puffs and being drawn back in, there is a fire present that is trying to find oxygen. If this information is missed, a backdraft can erupt, and that is a particularly dangerous situation for firefighters.

What became clear is that teaching agility is more involved than simply teaching a large variety of skills that can be accessed at will. Agility requires the ability to match an appropriate action to the specific situation. This implies an ability to "process" a situation accurately and quickly before any action is taken. For first responders, medical professionals, and firefighters, the honing of their "processing" abilities comes in the form of years of training followed by a career supported by training and continuous skill development. On average, firefighters train for 600 hours as part of an academy and then for two to three hours per day on an ongoing basis as part of their regular shifts.

## WHAT DOES THIS MEAN FOR SALES?

The highest-performing sales professionals understand that mastering agility is a process, not an event. This process is captured in the *agility enablement system*, which consists of three pillars: *situational intelligence*, *situational readiness*, and *situational fluency* (Table 6.1). The following three chapters address each pillar of agility in detail, but it helps to begin with a bit of context.

TABLE 6.1 **AGILITY ENABLEMENT SYSTEM**

| | |
|---|---|
| Situational Intelligence | Knowing what you need to know about the buyer's situation |
| Situational Readiness | Selecting the best course of action based on the situation encountered |
| Situational Fluency | Executing, effectively and efficiently, the chosen course of action |

*Situational intelligence* is knowing what you need to know. It is learning what characteristics distinguish one situation from another. It is the firefighter knowing what a chemical fire looks like versus an electrical fire. It is how triage nurses determine a heart attack from indigestion. And, importantly, it is knowing what works in each of those specific situations. How is indigestion addressed differently from a heart attack? Situational intelligence is based on knowledge—knowing the characteristics of the most common situations encountered and what distinguishes them from one another.

*Situational readiness* is the ability to select the best course of action based on the situation encountered. It takes the primary characteristics of the situation encountered and uses those cues to determine which actions will work best given the situation. It is focused on the skills and abilities that best match the most effective response to the situations you most commonly encounter. In other words, situational readiness focuses on selecting the actions that will most likely lead to the desired result. If triage nurses meet a patient having a stroke, they not only have the situational intelligence to know it is a stroke, but they must also be equipped with the skills to respond and to put their knowledge (or situational intelligence) into action to treat the patient.

*Situational fluency* is the bringing together of the situation an individual has encountered and the effective execution of the chosen response. It is creating and reinforcing the connections between what you "know" and what you "do" and eventually, reducing the amount of time between recognition and action. Situational fluency is what you witness in the emergency room when someone is wheeled in on a stretcher and the medical personnel all jump into quick, decisive action, executing their roles with confidence and competence. It is not enough to know a patient is having a stroke and know how to treat the stroke. The medical personnel must execute the selected treatment in a timely and effective manner.

## THE EFFECTIVENESS OF THE AGILITY ENABLEMENT SYSTEM IN SPORTS

Athletes provide the most visible example of the pillars of situational agility because we can witness it live while it is happening. No two athletes demonstrate this more effectively than Serena Williams, US tennis champion, and Lionel Messi, an Argentine football (soccer) star. And while fans of those respective sports may argue about whether these athletes are the greatest of all time (GOAT), most will agree that their demonstration of agility is exceptional.

Even if you do not consider yourself a sports fanatic, there is plenty to learn from the ways they demonstrate situational agility. Let's look at these sports lessons in the context of the three pillars of the agility enablement system: situational intelligence, situational readiness, and situational fluency.

## Situational Intelligence

We live in an age of abundant information, and nowhere is this more evident than in sports. Athletes and coaches have more sources of information at their disposal than ever before. They have information about their teams, their opponents, their own performance, the impact of different playing arenas and weather conditions—the list goes on and on. Intelligence is gathered through videos, wearable sensors, and optical trackers, to name just a few. Little happens on the field that is not gathered and analyzed. Imagine if all that data was provided to an athlete unfiltered. What would their reaction would be? Overwhelmed? Confused? Both! Data without an organizing framework to prioritize and contextualize is just noise.

Of course, professional sports organizations have staff dedicated to making sense of the data and using it to help equip specific positions and players on the team. Serena Williams knows a lot about the likely situation she will encounter before walking on the court. She knows which plays are most effective against her opponent. She knows how weather conditions, court type, and time of day could affect play. She knows the average serve speed and agility of her opponents.

Similarly, as a striker, Lionel Messi's focus is on scoring goals. He also knows the strengths and weaknesses of both his teammates and the opposing players. He knows which moves work against which players, and he knows the impact of the weather conditions on all of this. Both impressive athletes use their situational intelligence to make sense of what is happening in the moment, and that insight fuels what comes next.

The ability to recall the right information based on the circumstance, to recognize what they are seeing in real time and what it means, is one way the best of the best set themselves apart. Another defining trait is their eagerness to continuously add to and refine their situational intelligence. For Williams and Messi, this involves watching film, studying stats, and running simulations. Situational intelligence is not something you attain and store away. It is something you maintain and augment over time. Holding dear to prior assumptions about what does and does not work is potentially toxic to the agile mindset. Flexibility over rigidity is the path to agility.

---

**Holding dear to prior assumptions about what does and does not work is potentially toxic to the agile mindset. Flexibility over rigidity is the path to agility.**

---

## Situational Readiness

Situational readiness is the ability to select the best course of action aligned to the situation you are facing. The athlete who faces a certain opponent or pattern of play must choose a different treatment than they would if they were facing different circumstances. Situational readiness is having a range of options and knowing which options are best for each situation. It is situation-action alignment. How do you know which actions are best fitted to which situations? Experience and domain knowledge inform this situation-action choice.

We have been told all our lives that practice is what separates the highest performers in any discipline. And it is true but not as straightforward as we may have been led to believe. It is not just how much time you spend practicing. It is also how you practice.

Let us first focus on time. What is the ideal ratio of time spent at executing versus time spent practicing? Actual numbers vary, but a typical professional tennis player can practice three to five hours a day not including a gym workout. Messi is said to average five hours a day of practice. Those numbers do not include time refining their situational intelligence—reviewing films, studying plays. So, they practice two or three times more often than they execute. Is that the ideal ratio? Maybe, maybe not. Much depends on what you are executing and at what level you are aiming to perform. What does hold true is that practice is more time-consuming than execution, even for the highest performers.

**What does hold true is that practice is more time-consuming than execution, even for the highest performers.**

Readiness is also affected by what you practice. Which skills and abilities are most important for your field of play? Situational intelligence helps clarify what to practice. Serena Williams, as a singles tennis player, practices different skills than a doubles player might. Lionel Messi, as a striker, focuses on shooting and maneuvering through defenders. Practicing skills that do not lead to impactful execution or are not aligned to the situations in which you will need them is simply exercise.

**Practicing skills that do not lead to impactful execution or are not aligned to the situations in which you will need them is simply exercise.**

## Situational Fluency

The marriage of intelligence and readiness is fluency. Serena Williams recognizing how her opponent is reacting during a game and quickly strategizing based on her knowledge of what works best in reaction to her opponent's strengths is fluency. Her ability to factor in the "typical" play style of her opponent and aligning it with the actual game play is also fluency. Fluency is her adjusting to the changes in weather as the game progresses. It is Messi visualizing the path to the goal and outmaneuvering two, three, or four defensive players before he strikes the ball just out of reach of the goalie and into the net.

Fluency looks easy and it looks natural, but that is an illusion. Fluency is only possible with a sturdy base of intelligence and hours preparing to be ready to execute.

**Fluency is only possible with a sturdy base of intelligence and hours preparing to be ready to execute.**

*Success at anything will always come down to this:*
*focus and effort, and we control both.*
—DWAYNE JOHNSON, "the Rock," American actor

## SALES IS A LIVE ACTION SPORT

Not all disciplines require the type of situational agility exhibited by professional athletes. But sales does. Sales is the live action sport of the business arena. Sales is unique in its level of interaction and collaboration. Circumstances change quickly, new information appears, new players frequently enter and exit the field. Your best-laid plans are rendered ineffective without warning, and a new plan needs to be developed and quickly enacted. Sound familiar?

When looking at it in this context, it is not surprising that sales is often seen as a good career choice for former college athletes.[4] The difference, of course, is that unlike high-level sports teams, sales organizations do not traditionally focus on enabling sales agility. They focus on results and standardized practices. It is often the salespeople who ignore those organizational norms who excel—the ones who have cracked the sales agility code. Your high performers.

## THE HIGHEST PERFORMERS LEVERAGE TOOLS, NOT RULES

Let us reexamine the three pillars of the agility enablement system in the context of selling. Situational intelligence involves knowing the factors that combine to define the customers' buying situations you most frequently encounter. VantagePoint's research validated FSU's findings that most sales teams do not encounter an endless variety of buyers. Instead, they most often encounter four to six types of buying situations. Understanding those four to six types of situations allows salespeople to become faster and more accurate at assessing the situation in front of them. Of course, a customer buying team does not conveniently present themselves as a situation. And situations change over time.

This is where a distinction between rules and tools becomes important. A rule is a set of regulations or principles governing conduct for a specific activity. One could easily, and erroneously, conclude that there is a rule based on the four to six buying situations and the correlated winning sales strategy. It could be assumed that a rule is that if you encounter "situation 1, you should deploy sales strategy 3." While tempting in its simplicity, that approach would lead to mediocre performance at best. Why? Because the common situations faced are tools, not rules. A tool is a device used to carry out a specific function. Knowing that there are common strategies is a tool for more efficiently recognizing the situation a customer represents.

As mentioned, customers do not present themselves as "situations." Rather, they share some combination of factors that together paint a picture for the salesperson. This picture becomes clearer over time as more information is revealed, confirmed, negated, or contradicted. Understanding the common combination of buying factors that constitute a situation helps you know what to look for and how to make sense of what you discover.

To illustrate this, consider what happens when you visit your doctor with abdominal pain. There are hundreds of reasons for abdominal pain—just a quick search of WebMD will validate that! Through their training, your doctor knows that a common issue for someone presenting with your symptoms is an ulcer. Yet, the doctor objectively gathers information and checks symptoms to determine if that assumption is valid.

Doctors use their knowledge of how this common medical situation presents as a tool for determining next steps. If the doctors were not aware that ulcers commonly presented in a specific way, diagnosing your symptoms would take much longer and likely lead to more errors. Knowing the common situations makes the diagnosis more efficient, but it does not negate the need for diagnosing. Malaria can also present with abdominal pain. While it may be a much less common situation, a good doctor may inquire about your recent travels to rule it out before continuing.

As in medicine, customers provide salespeople with clues that can be used to identify their buying situation. Knowing the situations helps narrow an endless combination of factors into the most likely patterns, yet it does not preclude the others from mattering. Situational intelligence lies in knowing both the common situations and the situation factors.

## SALES PLAYBOOKS AS USEFUL TOOLS

Many sales organizations codify their situational intelligence in sales playbooks or persona-based tools. Many of these playbooks include characteristics of customers, their problems, and the recommended tools and techniques to sell to them. The intention of these tools is clear and beneficial—to help sellers make better, more impactful decisions that will lead to increased wins. Playbooks and similar tools aim to organize the collective wisdom and experience of the sales force and make it accessible to all. So, why with such a clear benefit and valuable information, do playbooks often fail to be used?

A part of the answer ties back to the difference between tools and rules. A playbook may be interpreted, or even described, as a rule, describing precisely what to do and how to do it. However, customer situations rarely follow the book. So, when there is a disconnect, the playbook is less valid. Playbooks may also feel restricting. Recall that sales is a live action sport. Salespeople need to be adept at responding in the moment, at being agile, so while tools that support their decision-making abilities are valuable, rules are seldom usefully deployed.

Another reason playbook initiatives often fall short of expectations is that they are often based on a one-size-fits-all sales methodology. In many organizations, playbooks are part of the effort to create standardization of sales efforts. As discussed in previous chapters, agile sellers are the ones least likely to follow a standardized approach.

To be clear, we are not suggesting that sales playbooks are bad. In fact, the best ones are excellent. The best playbooks document situational intelligence and lay the foundation for situational readiness.

## NOT EVERYTHING IS A NAIL:
## THE OVERRELIANCE ON SALES TOOLS

Situational readiness is being equipped to act with efficiency and effectiveness in any given sales situation. While situational intelligence helps a salesperson *know* what to do *when*, situational readiness ensures those tools are sharp and ready for action. This is another reason why the one-size-fits-all sales methodology approach falls short. It encourages salespeople to become over reliant on a small set of sales tools—those that reside within the sales methodology of their organization.

> While situational intelligence helps a salesperson
> *know* what to do *when*, situational readiness ensures
> those tools are sharp and ready for action.

As famed American psychologist Abraham Maslow said, "To a man with a hammer, everything looks like a nail." By focusing sellers on one set of tools, sellers become disproportionally skilled. This might work in a calm, stable environment in which customers and their buying situations remain ever constant. Does such a universe exist? By focusing on one sales strategy and the tools to deploy it, organizations unwittingly diminish their sellers' ability to respond to a wide variety of situations. And training the salespeople on one sales methodology is teaching them to be average performers, at best. Sales agility requires sellers to be prepared to use whatever sales tools are necessary given the customer situation. It also includes the ability to switch tools quickly as needed.

After an exhaustive analysis of sales literature, FSU's research group identified four core sales strategies that agile sellers move between (Figure 6.2). Through further research, 3 tactics were found to be most frequently aligned to each strategy. If you are doing the math, that means there are 12 sales tactics at the core of situational agility. Those tactics are a salesperson's toolkit. If you are like the seller with the hammer, there may be certain tools based on what you are selling and whom you are selling to that you use more frequently than others. However, that does not negate the importance of having the other tools sharpened and ready to use.

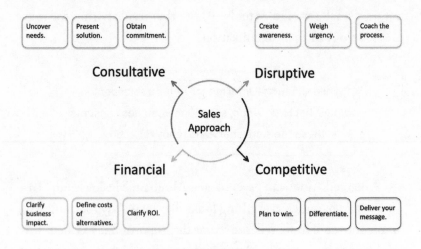

FIGURE 6.2 **Sales Strategies and Tactics**
*Source:* VantagePoint Performance.

Situational readiness requires practice, discipline, and coaching. It also requires prioritization based on situational intelligence. Situational intelligence helps organizations and sales managers to better understand which combination of strategies and tactics are most impactful when deployed in their common situations. Notice that we are saying "which combination." Although the research aligned certain tactics to certain strategies, this alignment is fluid, meaning that any of the 12 tactics may be used to deploy any of the sales strategies. More information on this is in Chapter 8.

## SITUATIONAL FLUENCY MEANS THINGS ARE CHANGEABLE, NOT RIGID

The word *fluency* is an apt descriptor of a successful sales conversation. It has several meanings including flowing freely, able and nimble, changeable, and not rigid. *Situational fluency*, the last component of the agility enablement system, is the execution of the right tools at the right time in a fluid and graceful manner. It is like a dance, in which the sellers are leading gently and with continuous attention to the needs of their partners. While executing, agile salespeople are also verifying the intelligence gathered in the preparation of a sales call, determining if the tools they came prepared to deploy are still the best ones, and adjusting as needed.

## SUMMARY

Agility in any field rests on a system, a process by which practitioners are trained and developed. The *sales enablement system* details how sellers master situational agility. This system has three components: situational intelligence, situational readiness, and situational fluency.

*Situational intelligence* is the gathering and organizing of information relevant to common buying situations. A strong base of situational intelligence provides insight on what information to seek and how to makes sense of the information gathered.

*Situational readiness* ensures that you, the salesperson, are ready to execute when needed. It is your understanding which of the four common sales approaches (consultative, disruptive, competitive, and financial) has the highest likelihood of success and your having the ability to execute specific sales tactics to bring that strategy to life.

*Situational fluency* is the efficient and effective execution of the right sales tactic given the customer's buying situation. It relies on accessing the right intelligence and then choosing to deploy the most aligned sales strategy.

The sales enablement system relies on tools, not rules. Agility is fluid by definition. The most agile sellers are not those who follow rules. They are those who make the best decisions and then are open to revisiting and revising those decision as the situation changes and new information becomes available.

## KEY TAKEAWAYS

- Sales agility requires the ability to match an appropriate sales action to the specific buyer situation.

- Sales agility requires situational intelligence, situational readiness, and situational fluency.

- Situational intelligence is not something you attain and store away. It is something you maintain and augment over time.

- Knowing the common buying situations you might encounter makes the diagnosis more efficient, but it does not negate the need for diagnosing.

- Situational readiness ensures that you are prepared to execute the sales approach that will have the greatest impact.

- Situational fluency is when situational intelligence and readiness empower execution of sales tactics.

## CHAPTER 7

# An Examination of Situational Intelligence

ave you ever been to a dinner party where it was obvious that one couple had had a big argument on the way over? Have you ever walked into a room and had the sense that you were interrupting something? Most of us have, which means most of us have had experience with situational intelligence.

In each of these situations, you used your senses to gather information. You noticed a tone of voice, the body language, or other nonverbal cues like flushed faces. You then used your knowledge of societal norms and the people involved to make sense of what your senses were telling you. Some people are exceptionally good at doing this—don't we all have a friend who can quickly and accurately size up any situation? They may have a gift or a talent for it, or perhaps they have just had more opportunities to practice than the rest of us.

Recall that sales agility rests on *situational intelligence*, the first component of the *agility enablement system*. Situational intelligence is not the same thing as information, but information is its fuel.

Sales is arguably the field most challenged by this flood of information. Sales is the revenue-generating function of an organization, so it makes sense that those who have information believe it is critical that they share it with the frontline sellers and their managers. Information about products, about services, about marketing initiatives, about customer personas—the list goes on and on. You never know what a customer may ask or may need, so, to be safe, let us give the salespeople all of it! The irony of course is that by overwhelming salespeople with information, we render them less effective. To modify a common expression, the road to confusion is paved with good intentions.

## INTELLIGENCE SHORTAGE

What salespeople crave is not information. It is intelligence. *Intelligence* is the ability to acquire and apply knowledge and skills. It is the productive application of information. Intelligence links information to a purpose that has meaning or value for us. Information is objective, while intelligence is subjective. Turning information into intelligence takes work. It is not a straight line.

> Intelligence links information to a purpose that has meaning or value for us. Information is objective, while intelligence is subjective.

Even though we often act as if the more information we have, the more intelligent we will become, it is not true. In fact, multiple studies have shown that information overload can decrease our ability to make strategic, well-considered decisions.[1] So, having too much information is not necessarily helpful, but having the right information is. And this is where context is important. Information without context is limited in its value. Is driving 65 miles per hour good or bad? On a freeway it can be too slow, but in a school zone it will get you arrested. The context makes the information about the speed useful.

When it comes to sales, we have two sources of context: our buyers and our offerings. Salespeople are equipped with a lot of information about their products and services—their features and their functionalities. Internal sales training departments focus much of their energy on ensuring that their sellers know what their offerings can do and whether their sellers can effectively share this information with others.

Organizations overachieve at building product intelligence, focusing too much attention on the offering part of the context equation. Product intelligence is an essential component, but when not complemented with situational intelligence, it feeds into a sales-centric view of opportunities—the equivalent of everything looking like a nail to the carpenter with a hammer (as discussed in the last chapter).

> **Product intelligence is an essential component,
> but when not complemented with situational intelligence,
> it feeds into a sales-centric view of opportunities.**

## SITUATION, SITUATION, SITUATION

In real estate, it is location, location, location. In sales, we believe it is situation, situation, situation. And to be precise, it is about the *buying situation*, not the selling situation. The selling situation is an important part of *situational readiness*, the second component of the agility enablement system. Situational intelligence is focused on the customer. Understanding what your common buying situations are gives you the intelligence you need to identify them when you see them, and to prepare yourself with the skills and knowledge to win them.

Once the researchers at Florida State University's Sales Institute documented that the highest-performing salespeople adjusted to their buyer's situation (see Chapter 3), it became clear that we needed to know more about buying situations. How different was one buying situation from any other? What information were high performers using to distinguish them?

For our purposes, a customer's buying situation was defined by the characteristics and circumstances that either directly or indirectly influenced the customer's buying journey. As part of their 2014 study, FSU researched the characteristics of over 1,500 sales opportunities across multiple organizations and found over two dozen factors that could define buying situations. They also found that, on average, five to seven of those factors combined to define a unique situation linked to changes in seller behavior. This was the situational intelligence used by high performers that led to high success rates. The highest performers assessed situations, understood if and how they were unique, and shifted their behavior accordingly. This study showed not only that high-performing salespeople were agile but that agility was based on situational intelligence.

From a research angle this was extremely useful information. From a practical, how-can-we-use-it-to-sell-better perspective, it was a bit overwhelming. Many sales organizations do not have the time or resources to analyze their buying situations and identify the unique factors of each.

VantagePoint sought to make FSU's findings a bit more practical. We were curious to find which of those situational factors identified were most often encountered and most intricately linked to changes in seller behavior. In other words, we wanted to know if some buying situation factors were more important to pay attention to than others. We discovered that of the over two dozen identified by FSU, 17 were found commonly across multiple organizations. This was a bit more manageable but not much.

## THE BUYING SITUATION FACTOR CATEGORIES

Undeterred, we began a qualitative review of the factors looking for commonalities or themes that could help organize and make them more useful to salespeople. We found that the 17 factors aligned to five situation categories that, when taken together, defined the majority of buying situations that sellers encountered (Figure 7.1). In the sections that follow, we list each category and some of the questions sellers ask themselves as they gather information about a customer's buying situation.

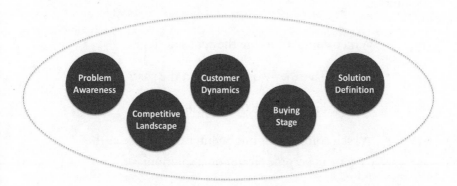

FIGURE 7.1 **Buying Situation Factor Categories**
*Source:* VantagePoint Performance.

## Problem Awareness

This category includes factors related to the problem the customers are facing and the degree to which they are aware of the problem and its implications:

- Do they understand the problem fully?

- Are they focused on a symptom and not the real issue?

- Are there implications of the problem not being considered?

Each member of the decision team may have a unique perspective on the problem and its ramifications. We explored how to use *pain questions* to assess problem awareness in Chapter 4.

## Competitive Landscape

This category encompasses the customers' current and potential relationships with others who can address their problems or offer solutions:

- Which competitors are they considering?

- Whom have they worked with in the past?

- How strong is or was that relationship?

- Which competitors might enter the picture as the customers become clearer on a solution?

This category also includes the biggest competitor you may face: the status quo. What about their current situation could tempt them not to act?

## Customer Dynamics

This is the largest and richest category of buying factors. It captures information about customers that may affect their behavior throughout the buying journey. It includes factors such as these:

- Demographics of those involved in the decision, such as names, titles, and time with company and/or industry, relevant experience, authority

- Motive for change, which may be different for each member of the decision team

- Relationships between team members

- Willingness to engage

As you can imagine, a customer with experience in your industry who is willing to engage and has a strong motive for change presents a vastly different situation than one with none of those things!

## Buying Stage

As a category, buying stage is the most straightforward. At what point in their buying journey did they engage with you? Or, at what stage have you engaged with them? Some potential buyers may not have begun their journey yet. You may engage with others while they are identifying needs and establishing criteria. It is more common than ever for customers to reach out mid to late in their buying journey, contacting you as part of a short list of potential vendors.

## Solution Definition

This category of buying factors relates to how customers are defining the solution that will address their needs. Some may have no idea what solution is possible, while others have one specific solution identified or may have identified selection criteria. Often, the later in their process that customers engage with you, the more likely they will have some sort of solution in mind. Given the wealth of good, but often conflicting, information that exists, customers may be clear on a definition that is not necessarily accurate. We explored how to use *gain questions* to uncover and shape the buyers' solution definition in Chapter 4.

## ASSESSING THE BUYING SITUATION

You may be thinking, "Those five categories seem like a lot of situation-focused information. Where is the situation intelligence?" Good question! Those categories represent the information you want to seek in any buying situation. You want to assess what you do and do not know in each of those categories as objectively as possible. But that is not enough. You also need to make sense of the information you gathered to create a cohesive and useful picture of the customer's buying situation. This process, assessing a customer's buying situation, involves two parts: seeking and orienting.

### Seeking

We have covered *what* to seek—information about the five categories of buying situation factors (as indicated in Figure 7.1)—so let us spend some time on *how* to seek. Many think the biggest challenge in seeking information is knowing where to look. In our opinion, the biggest hurdle is to remain objective while seeking.

As we gather information about our customers, we are tempted to filter it very heavily based on prior experience. A customer shares a certain problem or concern, and we begin mentally sorting which solution we will offer. Something we hear about their background starts us thinking about who the best reference for this prospect would be. We are guilty of this behavior. We hear a problem or opportunity, and we want to begin the process of addressing it. After all, we have heard these issues, opportunities, and/or desires before, and we know how to address them. We are being helpful and expedient. While our intentions are good, the impact can be losing, delaying, or minimizing deals.

We discussed buyer psychology and how the *righting reflex* (see Chapter 3) gets in the way of effective selling. True agility involves patience and skill at building the buyer's motivation to change, rather than jumping to solutions too quickly. Just because we know something doesn't mean the buyer is ready to hear it.

Earlier we shared that sales agility is a mindset, not simply a skill set. It is rooted in curiosity and empathy. It also requires a fierce commitment to reality—the buyers' reality. Your perspective on the buyers' reality and their situation is valuable and will come into play later in the second task of assessing (orienting), which is addressed later in this chapter.

For the first task, seeking, your goal is to stay objective, to gather information from the buyer's perspective. Why is this so important? Because your perspective taints your view of the buyer and affects what you seek. When you start inserting your perspective by identifying solutions or sales approaches while seeking, you often begin seeking information that confirms your gut instinct, and you don't go looking in areas that would contradict your initial ideas. When this happens, the consequences may not become evident until much later in the sales cycle. We run into objections or new and conflicting information and discover we were focused on a symptom rather than the customer's real problem.

Remaining objective requires self-discipline. Have you ever acted on a first impression or assumption that you were sure was right but was not? Of course, you have, you are human, which means you have biases. Our unconscious biases filter what we notice and attend to. The same happens in sales conversations. We are not aware that we are biased in what we are seeking, especially since buyers often reward us for shortcutting this process. Buyers are busy and often find the fastest route forward initially appealing. In the moment, the buyers may seem to appreciate the quick shift to problem solving, at least until they realize certain things are not being considered or your competitor does a more thorough job of understanding their buying situation.

It can be helpful to keep in mind that this is a case of slowing down to speed up. By slowing and focusing on what and how you seek, you create a solid foundation upon which to move in an agile way through the sales cycle. This may sound like common sense, but salespeople have traditionally been rewarded for quickly recommending a decisive action and for displaying unwavering confidence and an ability to convince others of their viewpoint.

Seeking in the way we propose requires a certain degree of humility, a level of comfort with not knowing coupled with the curiosity to find out. One of my favorite T-shirts has a saying that is relevant here: Do not always believe what you think. Look for evidence that what you think is true for *that* buyer in *that* situation. By assessing more slowly, you can choose and execute more quickly and more effectively.

### The Four Methods of Seeking

There are four broad methods of seeking information about a buyer (Figure 7.2). The first is the most obvious: *communication* (*conversation* in Figure 7.2). Having a conversation with the buyer focused on acquiring information related to the buying factors is the best place to start.

FIGURE 7.2 **Seeking Methods**
*Source:* VantagePoint Performance.

The second is *observation*. While conversation relies on what is being asked and shared, observation is gathering data through other senses. There is a lot of useful information in body language, work space conditions, and interpersonal dynamics. We had one customer who sold maintenance services to industrial sites who shared that their most useful source of information about a prospect was the site tour in which they could observe the level of cleanliness and maintenance.

The third category, *feedback*, is essential for sales agility. Feedback both within and between conversations with the buyer. Their comments and reactions, or lack thereof, are an important source of information that helps you refine and contextualize previously gathered data.

The fourth category is *research*. The first three categories require some level of interaction with the buyer; research is driven by you. What resources exist in your industry that highlight current trends or challenges being faced? What issues or concerns do others in your buyer's industry face?

All four methods for gathering information can add value and texture to the picture of the buying situation. Overreliance on any subset of them can frustrate or annoy the buyer and weaken the accuracy of the information you gather. Most often, communication is the source overemphasized. It is an extremely valuable information source, but it does have limitations.

For example, salespeople may overwhelm customers with too many questions that are of little or no value to the customers but are of significant value to the salesperson. Conversation, when it is not coupled with other methods, limits what you can learn about what the buyers know or believe. Without conducting research prior to having a conversation, you may miss the opportunity to understand how aware or receptive the buyers are to things that are relevant in their industry, such as emerging technologies or methodologies.

Ignoring subtle, or not so subtle feedback during a conversation can also have significant impact on the information you gather. For example, in one of our sales cycles, a salesperson did not pick up on a client's feeling that they weren't getting enough time with us. The questions the client was posing via email were an indication they needed more from us in reviewing our proposed solution.

The salesperson understandably read those questions as buyer preference for expedient email communication over live conversations. In a postmortem discussion on why we lost the deal, the buyer shared that we were not as communicative with her as she would have preferred. She didn't feel connected with us. By not being curious and seeking more about the buyer's behavior, we missed an opportunity to partner with them.

## Orienting

Assessing is a cycle of seeking and orienting, of gathering information and making sense of the information you have gathered. *Orienting* is what the most effective sellers do with the information they've gathered. Certain information may be remarkably interesting, even distracting, but it may not be particularly relevant to the buying situation of the customer. For example, we once encountered a buying team in which two of the influencers were in the process of getting divorced. That was interesting but not relevant.

In addition, one piece of information may gain relevance when viewed in combination with other pieces you have gathered. For example, we once learned that a junior member of the decision team, someone we originally believed had little influence, had attended one of our keynote speeches and was responsible for bringing us to the attention of her bosses.

If you envision the buying situation as a picture, the bits of information you gather are your paintbrushes. Your goal is to use those brushes to create an image that is as reflective of the buyer's reality as possible. This is where the second task of assessing (orienting) becomes important.

To orient, you must ask yourself questions using what you have gathered as your primary source for the answers. For example, is the decision team in agreement on what needs to be addressed? Do they have a clear and accurate understanding of their problem? What is their allegiance to your competitors? Depending on your industry, there may be questions to consider such as "What is the impact of their contractual obligations on their ability to act?" Orienting involves questions that you ask yourself, or your internal team, to layer the image you are creating and give it meaning. The more robust and accurate the image, the better sales decision you will make moving forward.

## SITUATION ARCHETYPES THAT FORM CUSTOMERS' BUYING SITUATIONS

As we have said, a specific customer's buying situation is unique and is composed of a variety of factors organized into five buying factor categories (problem awareness, solution definition, customer dynamics, competitive landscape, and buying stage). That does not mean, however, that trends do not exist.

In fact, VantagePoint was able to discern four situation archetypes—combinations of situation factors—that form the foundation of many customers' buying situations: *confused customer*, *bottom-line buyer*, *savvy shopper*, and *proactive partner* (Figure 7.3). These situation archetypes are tools, not rules. They are tools to help you orient and make sense of the factors that have the most significant influence on the buying situation. See Chapter 10 for specific information about the situation archetypes.

| Customer Situation Archetypes | |
|---|---|
| **Confused customer** | Customers have a **blind spot** around the problem, cause, solution, potential loss, or ability of providers. |
| **Bottom-line buyer** | Customers **trust my company** as a partner, know what they want, and want to **maximize their budget**. |
| **Savvy shopper** | Customers **know exactly what they want**, have a formal buying process, and are in the final stage of evaluation. **My company is on the short list** of vendors or suppliers. |
| **Proactive partner** | Customers **have pain, but they are uncertain or unaware** of the root cause and are **open to ideas and to collaborating** with me as a supplier or vendor. |

FIGURE 7.3 **Customer Situation Archetypes**
*Source:* VantagePoint Performance.

Remember our sports analogy in the previous chapter? Situation archetypes are the common defensive formations players study and learn to recognize during a game. The buying situation archetypes serve the same purpose: they help you recognize what you are seeing more quickly, but they do not minimize the importance of seeking and understanding the available cues.

## YES, SITUATIONAL INTELLIGENCE IS CURATED

You may be under the impression that this process of assessing, of seeking information and making sense of it, is a focus of early-stage sales conversations. You are right, of course. It is vital early in the development of an opportunity. It is also essential in the middle and late stages of the buyer's journey as well. Assessing is the process by which situational intelligence is developed. The more of the right type of information you gain over the course of the opportunity, the more useful the intelligence becomes.

And once again, mindset is as important here as skill set. Yes, you need to be effective at seeking information and orienting what you have found. You need to be skilled at questioning and timing and empathy and many other skills that come into play when interacting with a buyer. And you need to be flexible and curious. It is important not to be too attached to what you previously concluded, especially when new information emerges. Remain open to search for alternative interpretations that may fit.

Average- and lower-performing sellers rest on what they know and act on it with little desire to reconsider their conclusions as the opportunity advances. High-performing sellers are always assessing, looking for evidence that a shift may be needed. They are agile. They know that situation intelligence is not something that is created. It is something that is always being curated, and its value lies in its flexibility.

---

**Situation intelligence is not something that is created. It is something that is always being curated, and its value lies in its flexibility.**

---

## SUMMARY

Situational intelligence fuels situational agility. It is the basis on which you make sense of the buyer situation. Agile sellers *seek* information about the current buyer situation and then use that information along with previously gathered intelligence to *orient* or make sense of the situation. Our research has shown that there are five categories of buying factors that define a situation: *problem awareness*, *solution definition*, *customer dynamics*, *buying stage*, and *competitive landscape*. Agile sellers focus on using *conversation*, *research*, *observation*, and *feedback* as their methods for seeking.

VantagePoint's research identified four situational archetypes that represent common buying situations across multiple industries: *confused customer*, *bottom-line buyer*, *savvy shopper*, and *proactive partner*. These archetypes detail common combinations of buying factors, and they can be used to help orient the current buying situation. It is tempting to jump to orient too soon, to recognize something and assume that is all there is to see. When this happens, sales opportunities often stall later in the sales cycle as previously ignored priorities, decision makers, or competitors emerge.

## *KEY TAKEAWAYS*

- Situational intelligence is not simply information. It is information in context that can be used to help make sense of future situations.

- Situational intelligence is gathered over time and constantly added to and refined.

- Situational intelligence involves the seeking, or the gathering, of information through conversation, observation, feedback, and research, and it then involves orienting or making sense of the information. Situational intelligence helps you paint a picture of the customer situation.

- VantagePoint's research was able to identify four buying situation archetypes that describe situations relevant across organizations: *confused customer*, *bottom-line buyer*, *savvy shopper*, and *proactive partner*.

## CHAPTER 8

# Situational Readiness

It is interesting to watch sports with someone who really understands the game. The emotional roller coaster that happens when a tennis player misses an easy return or when a striker passes the ball that is easily intercepted by the defense is intense and often coupled by screaming at the television or leaping off the sofa. These experienced fans can see the play developing and understand the opportunities that exist, and it hits them hard when their favorite athlete or team does not take advantage of those opportunities.

Of course, these fans have the gift of perspective, of distance, of camera angles, and of replays. The athletes have none of those things in the moment. The athletes are making a series of decisions using their *situational intelligence* to determine what play or moves will most likely help them achieve their mission—a goal or match point. They are choosing to do what they believe will win in real time. The better and the faster they do this, the more successful they are. And those choices, the options they are deciding between in the moment, are a result of having spent hours, years even, becoming situationally ready.

Let's contrast that with Lisa Doyle's personal experience with soccer. Having spent years gathering what was basically situational intelligence related to soccer, she decided to join an adult recreation team. It looked like fun and a great way to stay fit. She understood field position and movement, ball handling, and how to recognize play development. After 12 years of helping run drills and practices as an assistant coach, she also understood what it took to be ready to play.

But all that mental readiness accounted for little during an actual game. She had no foot skills, coupled with a weak and inaccurate strike on the ball. And even though she was fast, she had very little spatial control, resulting in a lot of fouls (and several minor injuries). Arguably, she was situationally intelligent, but undoubtedly, she was not situationally ready.

Readiness means being prepared, which is a daunting prospect when you think about it. It is not as simple as knowing that when you see X, you do Y. That is just following instructions. *Readiness* is being prepared to do X, Y, or Z or A, or some combination thereof based on what is needed for the situation. It is having a varied and well-tended toolkit.

Let's revisit our first responders for a moment, specifically firefighters. They have the tools to gather situational intelligence in the moment as discussed in Chapter 6. They are also skilled and drilled on a variety of tasks from hose management to shared-air practices. And there are certain combinations of those skills that emerge as useful within the specific common emergencies they face.

For example, there are a series of related skills tied to responding to a car accident that are different, although possibly overlapping, from those required when responding to a house fire. The same is true in effective selling. Just as first responders pull from a well-tended toolkit, agile sellers do the same. In this chapter, we will explore this toolkit and the implications of the different tools at the salesperson's disposal.

## THE DIFFERENCES BETWEEN SITUATIONAL INTELLIGENCE AND READINESS

When sellers have access to *situational intelligence*, they have the tools to make sense of the customers' buying situation as it evolves. They are the quarterbacks who have the intelligence that is needed to make sense of the play that is forming in front of them. Situational intelligence is focused on the reality of the buyer's situation.

In contrast, *situational readiness* is why quarterbacks can successfully execute in that specific situation. They not only know what is happening in that moment, they also have an arsenal of plays to choose from. In sales, situational readiness also means having the right sales plays at the ready and choosing which of those plays and which of those tools best align to the specific buyer's reality. In simple terms, this involves knowing what the most efficient, effective, and successful sales approach is given the customer's buying situation.

The simplicity of the above formulation belies how critically important it is. What question do most sales professionals consider when strategizing an opportunity? Often, it is some version of, "What can we do to win?" or "How can we position ourselves as the best alternative?" While similar, these questions lack the perspective of the buyer. They are focused on maximizing the competitive strengths of the sellers. Which, of course, is the goal, but paradoxically, the fastest way to get there is to slow down (momentarily) and shift focus from what *we* need the buyer to hear, know, and/or understand, to what *the customers* want, need, and/or understand.

It is common to shortchange this process, especially if many of your buyers present with similar issues or your solution set is narrow. Recall what we've shared earlier: People like to buy. They do not want to feel like they're being sold. That feeling of being sold is often the result of shortchanging this process.

## THE FOUR SALES STRATEGIES

*Situational readiness* is matching the buying situation to the most appropriate sales strategy. We addressed how to understand the buying situation in Chapter 7 on situational intelligence. The other half of that equation requires understanding sales strategies and how they align to characteristics of common buying situations. It requires answering two vital questions:

1. What sales approaches, or strategies, are common across sales organizations?

2. Which of these strategies are most successful given specific customers' buying situations?

Fortunately, the research team at the FSU Sales Institute tackled this first question. Through an exhaustive review of the sales literature (picture a war room in which the walls were plastered with sales skills), we identified four patterns of selling behaviors, which we called *sales strategies*: *consultative selling*, *disruptive selling*, *competitive selling*, and *financial selling*. Each of these strategies is focused on accomplishing a specific sales outcome (Figure 8.1).

*Consultative selling* is focused on creating valued partnerships with the customers. *Disruptive selling* aims to address blind spots in the customers' view of the problem, the solution, or the market. *Competitive selling* highlights the competitive advantage of your

| Sales Approach | Sales Focus |
|---|---|
| Consultative selling | Explore needs with customers. |
| Disruptive selling | Reframe the customers' assumptions or beliefs. |
| Competitive selling | Position your offering above others' offerings. |
| Financial selling | Quantify the financial impact of your solution. |

FIGURE 8.1 **The Four Sales Strategies**
*Source:* VantagePoint Performance.

solution over all others. *Financial selling* is focused on illustrating how your solution yields the strongest return on investment (ROI).

Possibly, you are thinking, "Wait, but I do all those things for a single opportunity." We hope you do—when it is appropriate, that is. Recall that situations evolve over time, and assessing a situation is an ongoing process, so while a disruptive approach may be very appropriate early on, a financial approach may be a better fit as the situation changes. This willingness and ability to shift as the situation demands it is at the core of sales agility. It is why, as described in previous chapters, the one-size-fits-all approach to selling is a recipe for mediocrity at best.

## ALIGNING SALES TACTICS TO SALES STRATEGIES

We also uncovered three sales tactics that were found to align to each sales strategy, as shown in Figure 8.2. These activities represented the minimum of what was done in the execution of a specific strategy. We are not suggesting this is a comprehensive list—in fact, we know that it is not. Rather, these are the baseline activities that define situational readiness.

FIGURE 8.2 **Sales Strategies and Sales Tactics**
*Source:* VantagePoint Performance.

This is another example of the distinction between tools and rules. It is helpful to know which *sales tools* (that is, sales tactics or activities) align best to each sales strategy, but it would be a mistake to believe their relationship represents a *rule*. The relationship of sales tactics to sales strategies is fluid and not exclusive. This is a crucial point. While relationships exist, in any given buyer situation, any tactic or sales activity may be relevant even if it is not part of the chosen sales strategy.

Looking back to our sports example, there are defined plays that the quarterbacks are ready to deploy against a specific defensive position. The quarterbacks assess the situation and choose and execute the play that is best aligned to the situation unfolding on the field.

---

The relationship of sales tactics to sales strategies
is fluid and not exclusive.

---

Suspend reality for a moment and imagine that is not true. Imagine that quarterbacks are not ready to deploy multiple plays, and that they focus only on being ready to deploy one play that they use every time. What would happen? The defense would quickly figure out how to respond, and they would easily stop the quarterbacks' advancements. It would be crazy to teach quarterbacks, those facing the game action, to do the same thing every time. The best quarterbacks are decision makers, using the intelligence and tools provided to make real-time decisions, and they adjust those decisions as needed, in pursuit of their goal.

The highest-performing sellers are also decision makers. Therefore, the highest performers in any sales organization are those who most consistently ignore the one-size-fits-all sales approach deployed by their organization and choose one that best fits the situation in front of them.

Sales leadership and sales enablement teams often share with us their frustration that the best sellers often refuse to "play by the rules." Those sellers should instead be celebrated for doing that. They are choosing to match the customer situation with strategies and tactics that best fit. They understand that agility involves informed, intentional decision-making, not rule following.

## BUYING SITUATION ARCHETYPES REVISITED

In Chapter 7 we introduced four *buying situation archetypes*: common buying situations that cross industries. These archetypes are tools for making sense of the information you gather about a buying situation. As part of our ongoing research, we have aligned those common situations with the sales strategies most often affiliated with a successful outcome. This information is a tool for making a choice on sales strategy. Figure 8.3 aligns each situation archetype with the sales strategy that works best with it.

| Customer Situation Archetypes | | Consultative | Disruptive | Competitive | Financial |
|---|---|---|---|---|---|
| Confused customer | Customers have a **blind spot** around the problem, cause, solution, potential loss, or ability of providers. | | Strongly consider | | |
| Bottom-line buyer | Customers **trust my company** as a partner, know what they want, and want to **maximize their budget**. | | | | Strongly consider |
| Savvy shopper | Customers **know exactly what they want**, have a formal buying process, and are in the final stage of evaluation. **My company is on the short list** of vendors or suppliers. | | | Strongly consider | |
| Proactive partner | Customers **have pain, but they are uncertain or unaware** of the root cause and are **open to ideas and to collaborating** with me as a supplier or vendor. | Strongly consider | | | |

FIGURE 8.3 **Situation Archetypes and Sales Strategies**
*Source:* VantagePoint Performance.

As you can see, we use the term "strongly consider" because this alignment is simply another tool. Just as the archetypes themselves are not meant to minimize the importance of assessing, this alignment of situations to sales strategies is not meant to minimize the importance of choosing. It is offered as one more piece of guidance you can use to make the best decisions in the moment.

Like assessing, choosing is cyclical, and it is done frequently. Imagine you have prepared for an early-stage sales meeting with a prospect. You did your best to assess the customer's situation objectively and to make sense of what you found. You concluded that it was likely that this client had a narrow view of viable solutions. Based on the given information, you decided a disruptive sales strategy was best aligned. You prepared questions to ask to confirm her blind spot, and you also identified insights to share to begin to create awareness.

The meeting started off well, but then, before you could ask a single question, the customer shared that she had done a lot of research into potential solutions and had narrowed her best options to yours and your biggest competitor. What do you do? Do you execute the plan you prepared given this latest information?

Of course not. You quickly update your assessment decisions and choose a different path. In this case, you shift to a competitive sales strategy. And because you are an agile seller and have focused on situational readiness, you are able to smoothly switch as the moment demands.

## CONSCIOUS DECISION-MAKING OVER HABIT

These situation archetypes and the choices aligned provide a baseline for situational readiness. *Situational readiness* relies on making a *conscious and deliberate choice*, a matching of the buying situation with the sales approach best suited to it.

But let's be real: salespeople often do not make a conscious and deliberate choice. Often, they rely on habit, comfort (see more in Chapter 9), and organizational norms to choose which sales strategy to deploy.

> Situational readiness relies on making a *conscious and deliberate choice*, a matching of the buying situation with the sales approach best suited to it.

For example, I had a friend who, while attending medical school, was repeatedly convinced she had many of the syndromes she was studying (she did not). The same phenomenon happens after every new sales training—every opportunity seems to require what you were most recently exposed to. This is called a *frequency illusion*, and it is just one of the cognitive biases that can affect the conscious control we apply to our decision-making.

The most common example of the frequency illusion is that once you buy a new car, you begin to see that same model more frequently. The cars were likely always there, but your attention was focused elsewhere because that information had little value for you. The danger here is in mistaking reactions with choices. Why do we mention this? Because it is easier to react than it is to choose. And that is complicated by the fact that sales can be a game of speed.

## THE POWER OF THE PAUSE

Often, we perceive that whoever can respond fastest wins even if the solution is not objectively the best. So, the idea of pausing can feel counterintuitive and a bit scary. However, it can help to think of pausing as an infusion of oxygen, a moment when you are ensuring that you are choosing based on what you know and where you want to go versus reacting to the moment.

Taking a moment to make sure that the choices you have made are still sound gives you a burst of energy moving forward. The more confident you are in your situational readiness, the more options you have at your disposal, the more likely you will be to pause and use that time to make a more impactful choice.

This aspect of sales agility, situational readiness, is underappreciated and extremely impactful. The choice of a sales strategy based on a buying situation can happen very quickly, so it can feel less important than gathering intelligence or practicing fluency. Yet, the wrong choice can lead to wasted time and lost opportunities. Unwillingness to revisit and revise your choices is even more detrimental.

Readiness is the pivot point between intelligence and fluency, but it is not one directional. As intelligence is refined, readiness can be sharpened, and as fluency is advanced, readiness will grow. Situational readiness provides the confidence to choose and the flexibility to change your choice as needed. It is the power source of the *agility enablement system.*

Situational readiness provides the confidence to choose and the flexibility to change your choice as needed. It is the power source of the *agility enablement system*.

## SUMMARY

*S*ituational readiness is being prepared to act on *situational intelligence*. It is not about memorizing a predescribed set of actions. It is being ready and able to execute whatever actions are best aligned to the current situation.

Research has clarified that there are four sales strategies focused on specific sales outcomes: *consultative selling*, focused on establishing a deep partnership; *disruptive selling*, focused on challenging customer assumptions; *competitive selling*, focused on promoting your solutions above those of your competitors; and *financial selling* focused on clarifying and defining the ROI.

Each strategy comes to life through the execution of the core sales tactics associated with it. These tactics are not unique to a strategy, but they do represent core sales tasks associated with each. VantagePoint's research has clarified which strategy is most aligned with each of the situational archetypes first introduced in Chapter 7. Agile sellers are prepared to execute each of these strategies and move among them as a situation demands.

## KEY TAKEAWAYS

- *Situational readiness* is being prepared to execute whatever sales tactics or skills are needed for the specific situation you are in.

- While situational intelligence is *knowing* what to do and when to do it, situational readiness is being *prepared and able* to do it.

- There are four sales strategies agile sellers are ready to deploy: *consultative*, *disruptive*, *competitive*, and *financial*.

- Agile salespeople choose the sales strategy most aligned with the customers' buying situation. This process of choosing is cyclical, and it is done frequently.

- VantagePoint's research has shown that the four sales strategies are aligned to four buying situation archetypes. This alignment can be used as a tool for decision-making.

- Situational readiness requires a conscious choice.

## CHAPTER 9

# Fluency: The Most Important "F" Word in Sales

San Francisco is a beautiful city. It is also a city built on a very shaky foundation. Earthquakes are a way of life, and those who choose to live there have made their peace with the earth occasionally reminding them of the balance of power. Engineers have played a key role in minimizing the impact of earthquakes by creating buildings that are resistant to tremors. The buildings' foundations are engineered to move with the tremors as opposed to resisting them. Success was a result of redefining strength to include the concept of fluidity, a key ingredient in fluency.

Fluency, of course, is evident in human behavior as well. It is what we see and admire when witnessing exceptional execution. This is true regardless of the discipline: athletics, music, or specific professions such as healthcare, emergency response, or sales. Fluency is the hallmark of top performers in every field. It is achieved through practice—you do not become fluent by simply studying hard. There is a reason first responders and medical personnel are required to log hours of practicum experience before working on their own. Fluency is the marriage of intelligence and readiness. It is the outward expression of the hard work and preparation that is often done when no one is looking.

**Fluency is the marriage of intelligence and readiness.**

*Situational fluency* is the ability to deploy the right knowledge and the right skills in the right way at the right time. It is rooted in decision-making (*situational readiness*) and knowledge (*situational intelligence*). The term *situational* highlights that there is an external stimulus that needs to be factored into decision-making. Which means what is "right" is not static. Instead, it switches based on changes in the situation.

Situational fluency is not something one masters. It is something one must continually practice and play with, or it quickly dissipates. Have you ever stopped going to the gym for a period, perhaps due to an injury or scheduling conflicts? If you have, when you returned to the gym, you were likely dismayed at how much strength and flexibility you had lost that then required rebuilding. Like physical fitness, situational fluency is not something to which you can pay casual attention and expect significant results.

## THE IMPORTANCE OF CURIOSITY IN SITUATIONAL FLUENCY

Also, like fitness, situational fluency relies on a mindset as much as it does a skill set. As previously noted, central to this is curiosity.

The highest performers in sales and other fields are never satisfied for long with what they have accomplished. They consistently wonder, what else is possible? What if I tried doing it a slightly different way? What am I missing? A path paved by curiosity leads to impact. Curiosity prompts observation of what others are doing and consideration of new ideas and techniques. It is associated with stronger listening skills and a willingness to learn from others.

In her 2018 *Harvard Business Review* article "The Business Case for Curiosity," author Francesca Gino stated:

> When we are curious, we view tough situations more creatively. Studies have found that curiosity is associated with less defensive reactions to stress and less aggressive reactions to provocation. We also perform better when we're curious. In a study of 120 employees, I found that natural curiosity was associated with better job performance, as evaluated by their direct bosses.[1]

This ties directly to sales. You cannot be agile if you are tied too strongly to your own ideas, previous decisions, or sales methodology. As highlighted in Chapter 6 on situational intelligence, you cannot be agile if you are not curious about what else is possible, what the other person knows that you do not, or what you are not paying attention to that might be important.

## EXPERTISE VERSUS EXPERIENCE

Curiosity, and more generally an agility mindset, is also critical to the building of expertise. Expertise is not the same thing as experience, although they are often conflated. Having experience simply means you have done something for an extended period. Many of us gain experience at things we enjoy doing. You may be an experienced painter, dancer, or golfer. Your experience has likely given you a certain level of skill and increased your confidence.

In the previous chapter, we shared that Lisa Doyle was experienced with recreational soccer but far from an expert. Experience is achieved through practice and repetition. Simply doing something frequently is all it takes. Expertise, on the other hand, relies on a specific type of practice, coined *deliberate practice* by K. Anders Ericsson.[2]

Deliberate practice is the process of progressively increasing the difficulty of what is being practiced to systematically grow your competence. It is how professional athletes practice. They question, measure, and analyze previous efforts to determine how to improve, grow, and strengthen future efforts. They are actively curious about their performance and the possibilities of improving it; they wonder what else is possible.

---

**Deliberate practice is the process of progressively increasing the difficulty of what is being practiced to systematically grow your competence.**

---

Experience can create habits and comfort zones. Most weekend athletes enjoy their pursuits and want to maintain a certain level of competitiveness, but they are not pushing themselves beyond a certain point. They may be interested about what it would take to move past that point, but they are not curious enough to act.

Michelle Vazzana is an avid golfer and has maintained a 20 handicap over the past 35 years. Although she loves the game and plays often, her lack of deliberate practice has resulted in little improvement. She, like many of us, has reached a certain level of skill or ability and plateaued there. This happens in sales as well. Most sales organizations have some team members with a lot of experience but little expertise. They follow the rules, they use the taught sales methodology, but they do not strive to improve their sales skills. They strive to hit their number, and they are often dismayed when what worked yesterday in situation Y does not work today in situation X.

We all know salespeople who have been in sales for 20 years, who have gained a lot of experience and confidence, yet are not exceptional salespeople. They have an achievement mindset, focused on how they measure up against peers and metrics. There is nothing wrong with that, but it is not enough. The most agile sales reps, those who display situational fluency, focus on developing expertise. Developing expertise in sales agility requires self-awareness, dedication, and support. It is an internally driven process focused on evolving, not simply repeating.

> Developing expertise in sales agility requires self-awareness, dedication, and support. It is an internally driven process focused on evolving, not simply repeating.

Average- and lower-performing sellers rely on others, usually sales managers, to highlight how they can improve and grow. Highly agile salespeople use this input but do not rely on it. They are curious. They conduct their own assessments, take note of what they have tried and what has worked and what has not. They consider what else they could have done. They expand and strengthen their situational intelligence and readiness as they execute.

## YOUR CORE AGILITY MUSCLES

We have said that agile salespeople have a growth mindset—they try new things, develop new sales muscles, and work on balancing their strengths and weaknesses. To extend the muscle analogy begun in the previous chapter, sales agility requires a well-balanced musculature. Your "body" of sales muscles needs to be balanced so that you can rely on any one of them when you need it.

Ballet dancers are a great example of agility rooted in balanced strength. The control dancers demonstrate as they leap and spin is possible only when the body works in unison. Dancers are only as strong as their weakest muscle. Like other athletes, dancers know that it is the core muscle group, the abdominal muscles, that reinforce, strengthen, and give power to the limbs. A stronger core helps them leap higher, spin faster, and hold steady longer. The core muscles are not the "show me" muscles (at least for most of us). They are the worker muscles, the ones that do a lot but are often overlooked and underdeveloped. The highest-performing athletes understand the importance of maintaining and strengthening their core.

The core muscles of sales agility are *assess* and *choose*. These are the unseen practices, the decisions that are made, that lay the foundation for execution. Because they are not visible, they can be overlooked or shortchanged.

When you strengthen your ability to assess (to understand the customers' buying situation) and to choose (to match that situation to a sales strategy), you increase the power of your subsequent movement. As with athletic agility, training this core is essential for sales agility.

To extend this metaphor even further, if assess and choose are the equivalent of your core agility muscles, your limbs are the four sales strategies: *consultative, disruptive, competitive,* and *financial*. They too need to be conditioned and trained for maximum performance. "Core strength does have a significant effect on an athlete's ability to create and transfer forces to the extremities.... The core is the center of most kinetic chains in the body and should be trained accordingly."[3]

## SITUATIONAL FLUENCY = SALES AGILITY

Each profession manifests situational fluency slightly differently. In sales, it is manifested as *sales agility*: the ability to cycle through the four essential phases of the Sales Agility Code™ quickly and effectively: assess, choose, execute, and feedback (Figure 9.1). The Sales Agility Code is a manifestation of the *agility enablement system* specifically focused on sales.

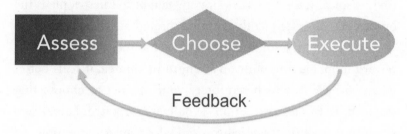

FIGURE 9.1 **Sales Agility Code**™
*Source:* VantagePoint Performance.

You may be curious as to why we call this a "code" and not a "model." We liken it to an operating system of a computer. Whether you use an Apple Mac computer or an IBM-compatible personal computer (PC), there is an underlying code that enables your computer to function. When everything is working well, you pay little attention to the code and focus on executing the task at hand. But when things don't seem to be working well and you suspect your computer has a bug or a virus, your focus shifts and you begin to hit the escape button or reboot hoping the system will correct itself.

When salespeople are using all four components of the Sales Agility Code, sales cycles hum and their focus is on executing the sales activities that move the opportunity forward. When salespeople ignore or overemphasize one component over another, things get buggy, and the focus often shifts to firefighting and saving the sale.

The component often overemphasized is *execution*. It makes sense really. Execution is what you do with the customer. It is active, it is visible, and it is gratifying. It is also the primary focus of most sales training and enablement efforts. Unfortunately, this often leads to an imbalance. Many salespeople are like weightlifters who focus on only upper body strength, making them disproportionately strong in one area. This is fine when the opportunity calls for that strength but disastrous when it calls for something else entirely. Typically, the first sales strategy taught to salespeople is the one they've most frequently executed throughout their career.[4]

And strength and comfort can become their own feedback-reward loop. Having built up strength in an area, it feels better when you use it, which reinforces your instinct to choose that strength. To be clear, execution is vitally important and deserves a significant amount of salesperson and sales manager attention. Yet execution is far more effective when balanced with assess, choose, and feedback. Since we've already discussed these elements in detail in previous chapters, we'll only recap them slightly here.

> Execution is far more effective when balanced
> with assess, choose, and feedback.

## Assess

*Assess* is the gathering of *situational intelligence* (see Chapter 10). Ideally your organization provides you with some level of intelligence—the personas that align to certain solutions, for example. Gartner recently shared that many organizations are now focused on technology to gather usable buyer specific data.[5] These sources of data can certainly help the process of assessing, but they are not needed to assess successfully.

Assess comes down to two things: *seeking* objective information about the customers' current buying situation and *orienting* what you gather to make sense of what you have learned. Sounds simple, yet most salespeople shortchange this process. They do not truly assess the customers' buying situation. Instead, they qualify the opportunity to determine if there is something to pursue.

We all know what this looks like, and most of us have been guilty of it. We ask the customers questions about their situation, and when we hear certain clues or indications that they are strong candidates for a certain solution, we stop assessing and start selling. This can lead to smaller opportunities, stalled deals, and frustrated customers. In Chapter 7, we reviewed the five categories of buying situation factors: *problem awareness*, *competitive landscape*, *customer dynamics*, *buying stage*, and *solution definition*.

Assessing is at the heart of sales agility, and it extends through the life of an opportunity. In 1992, the movie *Glengarry Glen Ross* made famous the ABC of sales: "Always be closing." This statement reflected the sales environment of the time, which was aggressive and adversarial. Today's environment is different. Customers do not want to be "sold." They want clarity. They want help. How do the most agile salespeople accomplish this? By following the ABA of sales: "Always be assessing."

## Choose

*Choosing* effectively involves taking what you understand about the customer situation and aligning it to the sales approach that will most likely lead to success. Choosing is the opposite of the one-size-fits-all sales approach. Instead, it is acknowledging that the best way to pursue an opportunity is to align it to the customers' process, not force them to follow yours. In Chapter 8 we gave an

| Sales Approach | Sales Focus |
|---|---|
| Consultative selling | Explore needs with customers. |
| Disruptive selling | Reframe the customers' assumptions or beliefs. |
| Competitive selling | Position your offering above others' offerings. |
| Financial selling | Quantify the financial impact of your solution. |

FIGURE 9.2 **The Four Sales Strategies**
*Source:* VantagePoint Performance.

overview of the outcomes of each of the four sales strategies, and those are summarized again in Figure 9.2.

Choosing happens quickly, which makes it challenging to do consciously. An overreliance on one sales strategy robs sellers of choice and can make them susceptible to the *frequency illusion*, as mentioned in Chapter 8. This thought pattern is a cognitive bias in which, after noticing something for the first time, we tend to notice it more frequently. Our attention is heightened in a specific direction.

For example, say you were recently taught a disruptive sales methodology and now every customer appears to have a blind spot. The danger here is in mistaking reacting with choosing. As with the assess step, choosing requires the discipline to pause and push against habit.

## Execute

*Execute* is the third component of the Sales Agility Code, and it is the one most focused on by sales professionals. It is when the strategy and tactic chosen are deployed. And while *assess* and *choose* empower stronger execution, the execution itself must also be strong and fluid. Sales success depends on assessing accurately, choosing wisely, and executing well. Agile salespeople can execute whichever sales tactic is needed, and they can pivot between tactics in the moment as new information becomes available.

You can execute without a strong agility core (assess and choose); average- to low-performing salespeople do it all the time. All salespeople execute. Only *the most agile* pay the same attention to assess, choose, and feedback. This is what distinguishes the top-performing sellers in every sales organization we have studied.

One more thing to note: an exclusive or overfocus on execution puts the sales process at the center of the opportunity. This happens frequently in organizations where a one-size-fits-all strategy has been deployed. This is the opposite of the buyer situation focus that is essential to sales agility.

To be clear, execution is critical. It is how you move an opportunity forward. Agile sellers need to be able to execute the four sales strategies and the tactics aligned to each. Each sales tactic is focused on achieving a specific sales goal that contributes to the outcome of its core sales strategy. Recall this alignment of strategies to tactics is fluid. It is up to each salesperson to choose which tactics will help them achieve a strategy's outcome for any given sales situation. See Figure 9.3 for an overview of the tactics and their primary function.

While execution of each tactic is unique, all tactics share a common foundation. Each tactic, to varying degrees, relies on a salesperson's ability to use questions to uncover and gather information and their ability to share information in an engaging and impactful way. In other words, each tactic rests on the salesperson's ability to seek information and share information.

Sounds obvious, right? Don't let that fool you. Common sense is not often common practice. A recent study reported that only

| Consultative | |
|---|---|
| Uncover needs. | Using a question-based approach to explore the dimensions of your customer's current versus desired state. |
| Present your solution. | Crafting your solution presentation as a story and delivering it in a way that will inspire your customer to act. |
| Obtain commitment. | Verifying the customer's commitment to buy by asking for a specific action to move the sale forward. |
| Disruptive | |
| Create awareness. | Challenging the customer assumptions, or blind spots, related to a problem or solution by offering information or a fresh perspective. |
| Weigh urgency. | Helping a customer weigh how impactful a previously unconsidered issue or problem is to their business and how it compares to other priorities. |
| Coach the process. | Coaching the customer on how to resolve a previously unconsidered problem by sharing the steps, processes, and best practices used by others in similar situations. |
| Competitive | |
| Plan to win. | Strategizing the key components of the deal, including the casts of characters, the deal drivers, the value link, the competition, and the customer's buying process. |
| Differentiate. | Identifying the ways in which your solution, your capabilities, and your delivery are unique and aligned to your customer's needs. |
| Deliver your message. | Using crisp and compelling statements that position and deliver your unique value message with impact. |
| Financial | |
| Clarify business impact. | Ensuring that you and your customer have a clear and mutual understanding of the desired improvements to their business. |
| Define costs of alternatives. | Quantifying the costs of alternatives to prove that your solution is the smartest choice with the best financial value. |
| Clarify ROI. | Calculating the anticipated gains from a solution (the return) against all the direct and indirect costs of acquiring it (the investment). |

FIGURE 9.3 **The Four Sales Strategies and Sales Tactics**
*Source:* VantagePoint Performance.

13 percent of customers believe a salesperson can understand their needs. That means that 87 percent of customers don't think salespeople have the skills to understand their situation.[6]

Seeking and sharing information are to the sport of sales what sprints and ball handling are to basketball. Michael Jordan is quoted as saying, "The minute you get away from the fundamentals—whether it's proper technique, work ethic, or mental preparation—the bottom can fall out of your game, your schoolwork, your job, whatever you are doing." Seeking and sharing are fundamentals used every day of a seller's career. And each salesperson chooses, consciously or not, whether they seek expertise in those things or are satisfied with simply being experienced. Agile salespeople choose expertise.

## Feedback

During execute, agile sellers are actively gathering *feedback*, the fourth component of the Sales Agility Code. Feedback is the thread that ties the other three components together. Feedback happens within and between each component, and it is the incorporation of new information into the process. This may prompt a pivot, a shift in direction. Feedback is a form of assessing, but rather than being focused on the customer situation, it is focused on the effectiveness of the decisions made by the seller.

Emergency room nurses provide excellent examples of incorporating feedback while executing. If someone presents with chest pain, they assess the likely cause and take steps to stabilize the patient. As they are doing this, they carefully monitor the impact of their interventions. If the interventions are not having the desired impact, they incorporate that feedback quickly and adapt their treatment.

In medicine and in sales, this *feedback loop* is an important source of information. Even inaction from a customer is a form of feedback. Customers who stop responding or who are frozen in the status quo are giving you valuable information about their buying situation. The most agile salespeople are always assessing and actively gathering and pressure testing their decisions and creating a clearer and clearer picture of the customer situation as the opportunity develops.

## Speed Matters

Up to this point our focus has been on what fluency—the dance between assess, choose, execute, and feedback—looks like and its essential characteristics. What we have not addressed is the need for speed. Sales is the live action sport of the business world, and, as in any sport, speed matters. You can have the best solution, but your competitor may get out of the starting gate faster and be able to influence the customer's decision process as a result. Sales success requires a balance of situational fluency and speed. Sellers who take too long to do any one aspect of the process will often fall behind their competitors.

The pressure for speed is sometimes cited as an excuse for shortchanging the agility process, specifically the assess phase. This is another area of distinction for top performers. They focus on agility even while under pressure. They understand that no decision is perfect, nor should it be sacred. They embrace the feedback loop and recognize that changes in direction are often a sign of progress. Being able to assess, choose, execute, and incorporate feedback quickly is a hallmark of the most agile sellers.

## SUMMARY

Fluency is what we see when the mind and body are working in sync to accomplish a desired outcome. *Situational fluency* is bringing to life situational intelligence and situational readiness. It is codified into the Sales Agility Code by four components executed by the most agile salespeople.

*Assess* is the foundational component, and it requires both *seeking* information related to the customer situation and *orienting*, or making sense of the information gathered. Assess involves both the gathering of situational intelligence on the current opportunity (seeking) and the application of previously gathered situational intelligence (orienting). Assess is focused purely on understanding the buyer's situation.

*Choose* is the selection of the sales strategy most aligned to that specific situation. It is the matching of selling focus to buying situation. Agile sellers choose among four strategies and then choose a sales tactic to deploy to advance that strategy.

*Execute* is when the agile seller deploys the chosen tactic and moves the sales cycle forward.

*Feedback* is the ongoing gathering of intelligence between and during sales interactions that may lead to a revisiting of any of the previous decisions.

This loop of assess, choose, execute, and feedback is the code by which agile sellers succeed.

## KEY TAKEAWAYS

- *Situational fluency* is *situational intelligence* and *situational readiness* in action. It is applying the right approach to the right situation effectively and efficiently.

- Situational fluency is achieved through deliberate and ongoing practice, which is how expertise is achieved.

- Situational fluency is unique in every field. In sales, it is demonstrated by mastery of the *Sales Agility Code*, which outlines the four essential components of sales agility: *assess, choose, execute,* and *feedback*.

- Execute is when sales agility is most visible. Assess and choose, however, are the core agility muscles giving power and strength to execution efforts.

- Each sales strategy has specific sales tactics that are executed in its deployment. While each of these tactics is different from the others, they all rely on the sellers' abilities to gather information or share information in an engaging way.

# PART IV

# SITUATIONAL
# SALES AGILITY

## CHAPTER 10

# Assessing: Gathering Intelligence on the Buying Situation

ave you ever made a New Year's resolution to get in shape or start living by a budget? Something you basically know how to do and want to do better? How often does the resolution stick? If you are like most people, until about mid-January. Your intentions are good, but you get distracted, or you turn your focus to other more satisfying priorities. Assessing the buying situation, which is the core of sales agility, often suffers from a similar fate. The seller has the intention to dig fully into the customer situation, but then gets distracted by something the buyer says that is clearly aligned to a specific solution and chooses to start sharing that solution's capabilities.

In Chapter 9 we introduced the concept of assessing, and we acknowledged that most salespeople understand the importance of assessing and that they execute it with some regularity. So, believing that assessment is a critical sales skill is not in debate. However, many salespeople routinely shortchange the assessment process, and as a result, they compromise their chances of successfully executing on their opportunity. Why? Because assessing is neverending and can feel quite daunting. Without some structure or framework upon which to rely, assessing can feel like fishing with a very wide net.

Assessing involves two sales skills: seeking and orienting. *Seeking* is the process of uncovering the information about the customers' buying situation. *Orienting* is the process of making sense of the story the information you uncovered is telling. Orienting, like all decisions we make, is improved when the information upon which the decisions are made is objective and thorough. That is not to say that seeking is ever "complete" or "done." Buying situations change continuously, and what was discovered previously needs to be validated and updated by what is true now. The most agile sellers know that seeking is iterative. We seek, process the information, and seek some more. Seeking needs to be balanced with action. Spending too much time on seeking can lead to frustration and missed opportunities.

---

*Seeking* is the process of uncovering the information about the customers' buying situation. *Orienting* is the process of making sense of the story the information you uncovered is telling.

---

## THE FOUR METHODS OF SEEKING

Seeking is an art as much as it is a science, and there are four methods: *conversation*, *observation*, *feedback*, and *research* (Figure 10.1). Questions in the context of a *conversation* with a buyer are an obvious and extremely important method for gathering information. Questions are addressed explicitly in two other chapters of this book (Chapters 4 and 7). They are often the most effective and efficient method of seeking, and it is hard to imagine a sales cycle that is not heavily reliant on questions. As with most things, however, too much of a good thing can be bad. Too many questions can be annoying or burdensome for the buyer, especially if those questions are data-gathering, low-value-to-the-buyer questions. Salespeople need to be strategic in the questions they ask and ensure that they are valuable to the customer as well as informative for themselves.

Conversation

Observation

Feedback

Research

FIGURE 10.1 **Seeking Methods**
*Source:* VantagePoint Performance.

Another way agile sellers seek information is through *observation*. In certain cases, this involves the physical observation of the business operations. What are the conditions on the factory floor? What does the desk or office of the buyer look like? In other cases, observation is more about interactions. How are decision team members behaving with each other? Who appears to have the power? What is their body language indicating?

Related to observation is the third method for seeking information: *feedback*. As opposed to observation, which is more passive and perhaps opportunistic, feedback is a deliberate focus on what comes back to you once you have done something. For example, how quickly does the buyer respond to emails? When you shared information about a specific topic, did the buyer show interest?

In addition, agile sellers balance the use of questions is by using another valuable seeking method: *research*. Researching the buyer's organization or industry is an important way to determine trends or issues that may be relevant. This research informs the questions they ask and helps validate their credibility to the buyer. These methods—conversation and questions, observation, feedback, and research—are interrelated and best when used in unison.

## WHAT TO SEEK: THE FIVE BUYING FACTOR CATEGORIES

As a reminder, situation factors, when viewed together, paint a picture of the customer's buying situation. The Florida State University Sales Institute's original research uncovered 27 factors that could be combined to define any given sales situation. VantagePoint's research allowed us to narrow that long list of individual situation factors to five categories to simplify and demystify the process of assessment (see Chapter 6 for research details).

The five categories are *problem awareness, competitive landscape, customer dynamics, buying stage,* and *solution definition* (Figure 10.2). In this chapter, in no particular order, we will discuss each of these categories in more detail and provide examples of factors within those categories and the ways salespeople uncover them.

### Buying Stage

This is the most binary of the categories since it is focused on a finite set of possibilities. Where is the customer in their *buying journey*? Are they at the beginning of their process, in the middle, or near the end? A typical buying journey, which has been defined in Chapter 4, starts with customers realizing there is a reason to change.

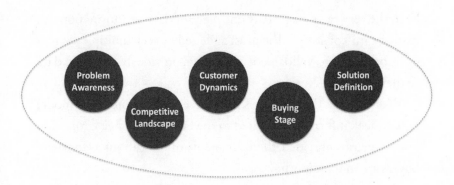

FIGURE 10.2 **Buying Factor Situation Categories**
*Source:* VantagePoint Performance.

In the early stage of a buying journey, customers may understand there is a problem that needs to be addressed or an opportunity to do something better.

In the middle stage of a buying journey, customers have begun to narrow down how they want to solve the problem or take advantage of the opportunity, and they are compiling their lists of needs and wants.

In the final stages of the buying journey, they are evaluating the best-fit options and choosing which to use to achieve their goals. Where buyers are on their journey influences their objectives and what they want from a salesperson.

Determining where buyers are in their journey feels like a straightforward process, yet it can often be a challenge. One reason for this is that buyers often do not have a clearly defined process in mind, so while they are in fact following a process, they are not able to articulate where they are in it.

The sellers' mindset can also complicate this process. Often, sellers make assumptions about the buyers' journey based upon limited information. For example, they may be contacted by potential buyers to discuss a certain product or service, so they assume the buyers are in the middle of their process when in fact they may be in the very early stage. Any one piece of data or information can easily be misconstrued. The most agile sellers seek multiple sources of information to validate, or invalidate, previously gathered data as they go.

We will use the scenarios introduced in Chapter 4 to model how to seek information related to the buying factor categories. In both scenarios provided, there are plenty of indications as to where buyers are in their journey.

In scenario 1, the buyer has received a directive from their boss to solve a pressing problem. In addition, the buyer has clarified solution criteria ("wouldn't require significant construction"), researched vendors, and set up appointments. These factors indicate the buyer is likely in the middle stages of their buying journey.

In scenario 2, there is very little indication that there is an active buying journey. The upcoming call is for the buyer to determine if she has an issue to be addressed. This indicates an early stage of the buying process.

## Solution Definition

This category focuses on the degree to which the buyers have *defined a solution* to address their needs or wants. Some buyers who are very early in their buying journey have not defined a solution at all. They just know that they want their problem to go away. Others who are later in their buying journey have a very clear vision on the solution they believe will help them move forward. Still others have some criteria but not a clearly defined product or service.

The degree to which the customers have defined their solution will have a significant impact on your choice of sales strategy. Often the more advanced they are in their sales process, the clearer the buyers are on their solution definition. That does not mean they are always right, however. Buyers may not be aware of the latest technologies or solutions on the market, or they may have a mis-conception as to their fit with certain solutions. As you orient, you will consider if the information you have gathered in other factor categories aligns to what you uncovered here.

**The degree to which the customers have defined their solution will have a significant impact on your choice of sales strategy.**

Applying this to scenario 1, there is evidence that the buyer has a vision of the solution based on online research and a requirement that it does not require significant construction. To verify if this is accurate, you might use questions such as the following in assessing this situation:

- I understand you did some research on QuietTech. What attracted you to our solutions?

- You mentioned that a low-disruption solution is important. What does that mean to you specifically?

In contrast, in scenario 2, the buyer had not considered a noise control solution at all. She was responding to an interesting conversation and just beginning an investigation process by talking to a salesperson.

Assessing in this instance may involve questions such as these:

- How have you been addressing noise issues to date?

- What is your familiarity with noise reduction alternatives?

In both scenarios observation may be a valid method of assessment in addition to the questions above. As an example, a tour of the plant may reveal physical attributes of the layout that could have an impact on possible solutions.

## Problem Awareness

*Problem awareness* is just what it sounds like. This category contains factors that indicate the degree to which the buyers are aware of their problems and opportunities. Like the solution definition category, this is a matter of scale. Most buyers are aware of what is and is not working on some level, but how aware and how accurate they are varies widely. Do they know the root causes? How clear are they on the ramifications of the status quo? Are they considering the price they are currently paying in terms of money, time, productivity, morale, resources, systems, and so on? How clear are they that addressing this problem will not create others?

In scenario 1 the buyer and their boss have done significant research into the problem and its consequences, and they have determined it needs to be addressed. Seeking questions such as the following may be relevant:

- I understand that the administrative staff's concerns prompted your investigation into noise issues. Which productivity metrics do you anticipate improving when the noise issues are addressed?

- I did a bit of research on the implications of a high level of noise in an office environment. One thing I was surprised by was its relationship to medical expenses, including increased sick leave. What implications are you most concerned with at this plant?

## Customer Dynamics

*Customer dynamics* is an extremely rich category of buying factors. Here you are seeking to understand the internal customer dynamics that may affect their openness with information and cohesiveness as a decision team. And since all sales involve asking buyers to make a change, you also need to seek evidence of their willingness to change and their motive for changing. Of course, you do not need to know this for just your main buyers but for all involved in making and influencing the decisions. As we all are painfully aware, misunderstood or unnoticed customer dynamics can derail a sales opportunity.

You might recall one painful example related to a request for proposals (RFP) response that we shared in Chapter 4. Our team believed the customers wanted questions and other communication to be done through email. After losing the deal, we discovered that they had been communicating in real time with our competitors, which contributed to a stronger relationship and had an impact on their final decision.

In scenario 1 there are several customers of which we are already aware. There is the logistics manager, the seller's primary contact, the plant manager who researched the problem and determined it needed to be addressed, and the office staff who are impacted by the problem and whose concerns prompted the plant manager's inquiry. You may seek to verify or gather information through questions such as these:

- What role will the plant manager play in choosing the vendor you will use?

- This process was instigated by the concerns raised by the office staff. How will they be involved in the process?

- How does a decision such as this one get made within your organization? Is it based on the recommendation of the main buyer, you, or are others involved such as procurement, HR, or legal?

Information about customer dynamics can also be gleaned from conversations with the customers. How they interact with each other, whose opinions seem to hold the most weight, whose are discounted or ignored. Of course, assumptions, as we have said, are dangerous. So, while it is important to notice these things, it is also important to verify what you believe you are seeing by continuing to seek through observation, feedback, and questions.

## Competitive Landscape

The final category of buying situation factors is *competitive landscape*. Within this category are factors that indicate the relationship of the buyers to your competitors. Do they have any relationships? How strong are those relationships? How integrated is the competitor in the organization? What contract terms are in place that could affect your sales cycle?

That is all clear from the title of the category. What might not be clear is the following: Who are the potential competitors? Those who could provide a solution but are not currently being considered? Considering these potential competitors up front gives you the opportunity to proactively guard against a last-minute addition to the "short list."

In many cases your biggest competition is not a competitor at all. It is the status quo. What do the customers like about the current state or status quo? What do they not want to lose if they make a change? Often, customers feel it is easier to accept the problems they have than to risk new ones.

In scenario 1, we know there are competitors being actively considered. In this scenario the following seeking questions may be appropriate:

- Who else are you considering for this project?

- How did you narrow down the list of whom you are meeting with to discuss solutions?

- I realize we are discussing solving your noise issues more wholistically, but I know that noise is not a new concern. I am wondering what you are doing now that you want to continue doing?

This category is one where research is essential. Your knowledge of your industry and competitors can help you identify areas that will, eventually, help you position your solution favorably. According to Gartner research, sellers who actively guide customers and help them assimilate and make sense of competing alternatives outperform sellers who overlook this critical element of the customer's buying journey.[1]

## ORIENTING: ALIGNING INFORMATION WITH THE CUSTOMER BUYING SITUATION

Seeking, using the five buying factor categories, helps to ensure that you gather a lot of relevant and objective information about the customer's buying situation. Orienting is what helps sellers coalesce the information they've gathered into a useful picture of the situation. *Orienting* is defined as aligning or positioning relative to a specified position.

> Orienting is what helps sellers coalesce the information they've gathered into a useful picture of the situation.

For our purposes, the specified position is the customers' buying situation; their reality is the point around which all the information sought needs to align. When you orient, you determine how this information fits together. You discover which pieces are important in creating a picture, which pieces are supplemental, and which are distracting. The more thorough and effective your seeking is, the more information you will be able to draw upon to create a picture of the customer's buying situation.

We previously discussed the dangers of making assumptions when it comes to assessing a customer's situation. This reflects the temptation to shortchange the process because it feels similar to situations you have encountered previously. When orienting, the challenge to remain objective is particularly hard. Orienting requires decision-making, which by its nature is subjective. You are deciding which pieces of information hold the most weight.

These decisions are often based on your prior experiences and the lessons you have learned from peers. You are applying your mental frame, the thought process by which you make sense of the world, to the information you have gathered. If your frame is faulty, based on assumptions that are not accurate, you will likely reach flawed conclusions.

This is one of the reasons why having a code, or decision-making framework, is so important. A code gives you structure and a process to follow. The Sales Agility Code is focused on delineating the decisions that are often made so quickly they are indistinguishable. And there are no decisions more impactful than the ones made while orienting. The output of orienting is a snapshot of the current buying situation. This is critical since it is the basis of your choice of sales approach.

> The output of orienting is a snapshot of the current buying situation. This is critical since it is the basis of your choice of sales approach.

This is not to say that the wisdom you and your organization have gathered is not a valuable resource for orienting—it absolutely is! The situational intelligence gathered on the most common buying situations you encounter is a valuable input into the orienting process. Data gathered internally may clarify, for example, that most customers you successfully partner with hold technology roles and are very informed about the services and products available. Many organizations use personas to organize the role-based situational intelligence they have gathered. These are great resources to help with orienting. Matching those resources with the information gathered while seeking helps create a strong basis for your assessment conclusions.

Of course, not all organizations have situational intelligence codified or use personas to target specific types of buyers. In those cases, salespeople are often left up to their own devices to make sense of the situational information they have gathered. Admittedly some salespeople are excellent at this. They possess an agile mindset of intelligence and objectivity, and they question their own decisions as they go along. Others need more support.

VantagePoint has created a resource for those who need or want additional situational intelligence. One of the services we provide is a diagnostic process that analyzes the common situations our customers' sellers encounter, and it creates snapshots of the most common ones. This provides very specific situational intelligence to the customers we support. Not every organization has the resources or a large enough sales organization to undergo this diagnostic process.

## COMMON ARCHETYPES OF BUYING SITUATIONS

Because diagnostics are not a fit for every customer, we got curious and began to wonder if themes would emerge if we looked across all the data, regardless of industry or organization. What we found was that there are four common archetypes of buying situations that are relevant to most companies. An *archetype* is a combination of situation factors that combine to create a customer buying situation. They serve as an input into the orienting process.

These archetypes are like the outer edge of a jigsaw puzzle; they give you a frame in which you will add detail and color. We have decided to give each archetype a descriptive name for ease of reference. There is nothing precious about the names, and many of our customers choose to rename them to something that resonates more strongly with their teams. The four *buying situation archetypes* that were uncovered in VantagePoint research are the *confused customer*, *bottom-line buyer*, *savvy shopper*, and *proactive partner* (Figure 10.3).

| Customer Situation Archetypes | |
| --- | --- |
| Confused customer | Customers have a **blind spot** around the problem, cause, solution, potential loss, or ability of providers. |
| Bottom-line buyer | Customers **trust my company** as a partner, know what they want, and want to **maximize their budget**. |
| Savvy shopper | Customers **know exactly what they want**, have a formal buying process, and are in the final stage of evaluation. **My company is on the short list** of vendors or suppliers. |
| Proactive partner | Customers **have pain, but they are uncertain or unaware** of the root cause and are **open to ideas and to collaborating** with me as a supplier or vendor. |

FIGURE 10.3 **Customer Situation Archetypes**
*Source:* VantagePoint Performance.

Let's see how these archetypes line up to the two fictional scenarios we have been using. In scenario 1, the buyer has done significant research and has created a short list of vendors to engage with. They most align to the savvy shopper archetype although it is unclear if they have a formalized buying process or are truly late stage. These are things you would need to continue to assess as you execute and, if warranted, update your decisions based on what you learn.

In scenario 2, the buyer is very early stage, not really in a buying journey at all. She is just gathering information. From what you know right now, she most aligns with proactive partner. She is reaching out for your guidance and support based on your successful relationship with someone she trusts. Again, this assessment of her situation may need to be updated as you learn more through the sales cycle.

## SUMMARY

Agile sellers are master decision makers at their core. And nowhere is their decision-making more important than in the assessment of the customer situation. *Assess*, the first component of the Sales Agility Code framework, consists of two distinct skills: seeking and orienting.

*Seeking* is gathering objective information on the buyer's situation. We have shared five categories of buying factors that help organize seeking and ensure that a complete picture is sought. Those categories are the buying stage, *problem awareness*, *solution definitions*, *customer dynamics*, and *competitive landscape*.

> *Research is useful until it becomes a form of procrastination.*
> —JAMES CLEAR, *Atomic Habits*

Once as much information as is reasonable is gathered, agile sellers *orient*—that is, they make sense of the information they have gathered. They put the information in context and look for themes using their past experience as a tool for understanding the picture that has emerged. We have shared *buying situation archetypes* that can be used to help orient common situations that cross organizations and industries.

As you assess, you are building *situational intelligence*. As your base of situational intelligence grows, your ability to be agile expands. Agile sellers are always assessing.

# KEY TAKEAWAYS

- Assessing involves both seeking information and orienting or making sense of the information gathered.

- The ability to consistently assess well is a differentiator between higher-performing salespeople and their peers. The motto of an agile salesperson is, "Always be assessing."

- Seeking involves gathering information on the five buying factor categories through *questions asked in conversations*, *research*, *observation*, and *feedback*. The categories are *problem awareness, solution definition, customer dynamics, competitive landscape*, and *buying stage*.

- *Orienting* is combing through all of the information gathered in the categories above to create a cohesive picture of the customer situation that is as complete as possible. Agile sellers use situational intelligence to decide which pieces of information gathered hold the most weight.

- VantagePoint uncovered four *buying situation archetypes* that can be used to make sense of a customer buying situation: *confused customer, bottom-line customer, savvy shopper*, and *proactive partner*. They represent common combinations of situation factors across industries.

## CHAPTER 11

# Choosing and Executing Situational Sales Agility

How many choices do you think you make in an average day? You may be surprised that several research studies have estimated that the average adult makes 35,000 decisions each day.[1] And if that is the average, it is safe to say that there are lots of choices we make often without thinking deeply about them. This is fine for relatively small decisions such as what to wear to work or how large a coffee to order, but it is riskier when we start making more impactful decisions without giving them the attention they deserve. We see this all the time in the business world: "This is the way we have always done it" is a common way we let ourselves avoid conscious choices. It is a tempting way of thinking especially when we are being encouraged to "stay the course" or be a team player.

As you read in Chapter 6, *conscious choice* is the most significant distinguisher between high-performing salespeople and their lower-performing peers. High-performing sellers varied their sales approach based on the situation they faced, versus average and low performers who used the same approach regardless of changes in the buying situation. And while high performers are celebrated for their results, they are often casually maligned for their methods.

Many of the organizations with which we work describe their highest performers as "cowboys" or "mavericks," telling us that they do not respond to training initiatives and are not held accountable to them. They are left alone to do what they want because they get results. These same organizations adopt a sales methodology, the "Acme-way of selling," that purportedly provides a sales path and narrows the decisions sellers need to make. While the intentions are good, the thinking is flawed. If they want more salespeople to be top performers, why ask them to behave in a way their top performers reject?

It is the *choose* step within the Sales Agility Code that captures this characteristic of high-performing salespeople. This is the step you are taking when you match the output of your assessment to a sales strategy and, subsequently, the appropriate sales tactics to execute. It is the bridge between understanding and doing. Of course, all salespeople choose what they will do based on whatever level of assessment they conduct. And like the assess step, it is not *if* you do it but *how* you do it.

A sales strategy defines a specific path to the desired sales outcome. The goal of the choose step is to pick the strategy most aligned to the buying situation. If your choice is limited to one sales strategy, there is no choice to be made. Agile salespeople know there is more than one choice. They make a conscious choice of strategy based on their assessment of the situation, resulting in better buying experiences and stronger win rates.

Consciously choosing a sales strategy is not only beneficial to the salesperson. It is also more reflective of the customers' buying journey. If customers are well into their buying journey and trying to make a choice from among the solutions they have researched, they would be annoyed by a salesperson who wanted to apply the *consultative selling strategy* and do deep discovery. Those customers would be better suited to a *competitive strategy*, focused on highlighting the seller's competitive advantages.

The sales strategy helps establish the goals of the sales process. It is a strategic choice about what needs to be accomplished with the customer to advance the opportunity. You will also make a more tactical choice about which sales tactics to deploy in the execution of that strategy. We address this choice separately later in the chapter.

## CHOOSE: THE FOUR SALES STRATEGIES

Agile sellers make the best decision they can at the time, based on the objective picture they have created of the customer buying situation, knowing that this choice may change as more information becomes available and the picture evolves. There are four sales strategies, each with a core sales objective:

- *Consultative:* Establish a trusted partnership and help customers uncover needs.

- *Disruptive:* Reframe the customers' assumptions around their problem and its implications, or possible solutions.

- *Competitive:* Position the advantages of your solutions.

- *Financial:* Quantify purchase considerations.

As discussed in Chapter 2, *consultative* is a foundational sales strategy that underpins the other three. It can be the only one used in a sales cycle, or it can be used in combination with one or two others. The choice of sales strategy is not a one-time event. It is open to reconsideration as you gather and incorporate more information into your previous assessment decisions.

In Chapter 10 we discussed the *buying situation archetypes* that summarized the common buying situations that have emerged through VantagePoint's research. These archetypes are also found to align with specific sales strategies as shown in Figure 11.1. As you can see, the factors that shape the situation are closely aligned to the most effective sales strategy.

| Customer Situation Archetypes | | Consultative | Disruptive | Competitive | Financial |
|---|---|---|---|---|---|
| **Confused customer** | Customers have a **blind spot** around the problem, cause, solution, potential loss, or ability of providers. | | Strongly consider | | |
| **Bottom-line buyer** | Customers **trust my company** as a partner, know what they want, and want to **maximize their budget**. | | | | Strongly consider |
| **Savvy shopper** | Customers **know exactly what they want**, have a formal buying process, and are in the final stage of evaluation. **My company is on the short list** of vendors or suppliers. | | | Strongly consider | |
| **Proactive partner** | Customers **have pain, but they are uncertain or unaware** of the root cause and are **open to ideas and to collaborating** with me as a supplier or vendor. | Strongly consider | | | |

FIGURE 11.1 **Situation Archetypes and Sales Strategies**
*Source:* VantagePoint Performance.

Let's see how the process of choosing might play out for our two fictional scenarios introduced in the previous chapters. In scenario 1, the buyer has already done quite a bit of research and has narrowed options down to a few companies, including QuietTech. Your best path to a win here is to position the advantages of your solution over any potential competitors. For that reason, a competitive sales strategy is most appropriate. In scenario 2, you are working with a potential buyer who is very early stage and in the process of gathering information to determine if there truly is a noise problem to solve. For those reasons, a consultative strategy would be most aligned. You want to establish yourself as a trusted resource to help her navigate her investigation and eventual purchase.

## DETERMINING HOW TO DEPLOY THE CHOSEN STRATEGY

Once you've chosen a strategy in alignment with your assessment, you need to make another important choice: what will you do to deploy that strategy? In Chapter 6 we introduced the sales tactics that align to each sales strategy. Figure 11.2 illustrates that relationship.

| Consultative | |
|---|---|
| Uncover needs. | Using a question-based approach to explore the dimensions of your customer's current versus desired state. |
| Present your solution. | Crafting your solution presentation as a story and delivering it in a way that will inspire your customer to act. |
| Obtain commitment. | Verifying the customer's commitment to buy by asking for a specific action to move the sale forward. |
| **Disruptive** | |
| Create awareness. | Challenging the customer assumptions, or blind spots, related to a problem or solution by offering information or a fresh perspective. |
| Weigh urgency. | Helping a customer weigh how impactful a previously unconsidered issue or problem is to their business and how it compares to other priorities. |
| Coach the process. | Coaching the customer on how to resolve a previously unconsidered problem by sharing the steps, processes, and best practices used by others in similar situations. |
| **Competitive** | |
| Plan to win. | Strategizing the key components of the deal, including the casts of characters, the deal drivers, the value link, the competition, and the customer's buying process. |
| Differentiate. | Identifying the ways in which your solution, your capabilities, and your delivery are unique and aligned to your customer's needs. |
| Deliver your message. | Using crisp and compelling statements that position and deliver your unique value message with impact. |
| **Financial** | |
| Clarify business impact. | Ensuring that you and your customer have a clear and mutual understanding of the desired improvements to their business. |
| Define costs of alternatives. | Quantifying the costs of alternatives to prove that your solution is the smartest choice with the best financial value. |
| Clarify ROI. | Calculating the anticipated gains from a solution (the return) against all the direct and indirect costs of acquiring it (the investment). |

FIGURE 11.2  **The Four Sales Strategies and Sales Tactics**
*Source:* VantagePoint Performance.

As we said in Chapter 6, this is a tool, not a rule. The alignment of tactics to strategies is fluid, meaning that any tactic can be deployed in the service of any strategy depending upon the situation. The three listed in the figure are most commonly involved, but rarely are they the only tactics used in deploying the strategy. Each sales tactic is focused on accomplishing a specific sales task related to the overall outcome of its related strategy.

This, as you have likely surmised, is not a comprehensive list of sales tactics. It is a place to start, and we encourage you not to limit yourself. Each sales organization is unique, and yours may have tactics to add to this list that reflect what you sell and to whom you sell it. Likewise, some organizations rely on a smaller set of tactics, and perhaps they do not focus on financial selling, for example. Also, it bears repeating that consultative is foundational, and *consultative tactics* are likely deployed to some degree in executing each of the other three strategies. For example, it is hard to imagine a sales cycle in which you did not have to present your solution!

> Consultative is foundational, and *consultative tactics*
> are likely deployed to some degree in
> executing each of the other three strategies.

How do agile sellers narrow down which tactics to deploy in pursuit of their chosen strategy? You likely know the answer to that by now: they use the information they have gathered through assessment to determine the best next step for the specific buying situation.

Let's see how that looks in our two scenarios. In scenario 1, for which we have chosen the competitive strategy, we may focus on *differentiate* since we know we are in direct competition with a select group of vendors. To stay in consideration, we need to highlight the unique attributes of our solution and how they benefit the buyer.

In scenario 2, the buying journey has barely begun. One possible choice is to *uncover needs* and help the buyer to fully understand any implications of their current noise management procedures.

Another possibility is to *create awareness* and then *uncover needs*. In the noise management arena, buyers are largely unaware of advancements in the technology. In this case, choosing to disrupt their thinking about the impact of noise on productivity may open them up to understanding the need and potential solutions more clearly. In essence, you have chosen to add this *disruptive tactic* to the *consultative strategy*.

## EXECUTING THE CHOSEN PATH

You may be thinking that 12 tactics seem like a lot to learn and master. We hear that frequently from customers interested in partnering with VantagePoint. And, of course, they are right, 12 tactics seems like a lot. However, while each of the tactics is unique in its expression, they share a common set of skills and behaviors at their core. By focusing on those commonalities, agile sellers can equip themselves with the tools they need and adapt their application as needed.

The commonalities are the ability to seek information effectively and to give information in an engaging and impactful manner. Most of the tactics rely more heavily on one than the other. For example, *create awareness* is more focused on giving than seeking, while *uncover needs* is more focused on seeking.

### Tactic Execution: Seeking

*Seeking* is pursuing specific information related to the advancement of the sales strategy. Seeking as part of a sales tactic execution is different from seeking to assess a buyer's situation. It involves the same core skills that assessment requires—asking questions, conducting research, observation, and feedback. Yet, instead of using those tools to create a wholistic picture of the customer situation, you are using them to accomplish a specific sales task.

There are three categories of questions that are useful for influencing the buying situation: *background, pain,* and *gain questions* (Figure 11.3). These questions were first introduced in Chapter 4:

> *Background questions* are general questions that help you understand the circumstances. *Pain questions* seek to uncover the obstacles and losses that the buyer is experiencing. *Gain questions* clarify what the buyer will achieve by choosing your solution.

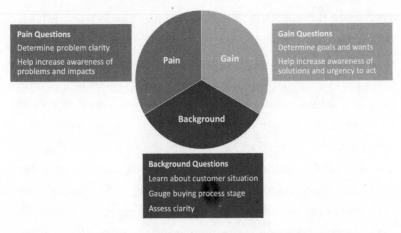

FIGURE 11.3  **Questions for Influencing Buying Situation**
*Source:* VantagePoint Performance.

Through your use of questions, you are trying to accomplish two important things in addition to gathering information. First, you are trying to understand the motives and priorities of your buyers. Why are they considering a change? What initiated this buying journey? What is important to them? Understanding the motives of your buyers will significantly affect how you give information when the time comes.

Second, questions help you build urgency in the mind of the buyers. Recall that we all like our own ideas best, and we often buy for emotional reasons and look for rational justifications (see Chapter 3). *Pain questions* help clarify and expand the opportunity cost for maintaining the status quo, while *gain questions* help customers articulate the upsides of change. Well-crafted *gain questions* help customers solidify the buying criteria and can help promote the unique characteristics of your solution.

Let's see how these questions might be used in the fictional scenarios we have been tracking. In scenario 1, you are meeting with a well-informed customer who has narrowed a list of potential suppliers. You have chosen the *competitive strategy* and plan to deploy the *differentiate tactic*. Before you highlight your solutions, you may want to ask some of the following questions:

> *Background question:* You mentioned that you are seeking a solution that can be deployed with minimal disruption. Quite often that indicates that a tech-based solution is the best fit. What is currently in place to support that approach?

> *Pain question:* The concerns of the office staff prompted this process. I am curious, what other consequences of the current noise level have you noticed that you'd like to see addressed?

> *Gain question:* How would having the ability to adjust the application of the noise dampening per zone help your staff?

In scenario 2, the buyer is very early stage and seeking to determine if she wants to initiate a buying journey. You have chosen the consultative approach, and you have narrowed your tactics down to *uncover needs* or perhaps *create awareness*. Below are some possible questions for this conversation:

> *Background question (uncover needs):* What is going on at your plant that makes you think there may be a noise control issue?

> *Pain question (uncover needs):* What impacts do you believe the current noise level is having on your employees?

> *Pain question (create awareness):* I came across an article detailing noise levels in production plants and the various ways productivity is affected as noise increases. I brought a copy in case you haven't seen it. One thing I found surprising was how productivity dipped in adjacent spaces. Have you seen any indications of this in your plant?

> *Gain question (uncover needs):* I realize you are in the beginning of your process, but I am curious. What are some of the attributes you might want in a noise control solution?

Agile sellers use questions strategically to build rapport, create interest, enhance curiosity, and establish trust. It is easy to fall into the trap of asking questions for your own benefit and forgetting to focus on the customer experience.

## Tactic Execution: Giving

You provide information to your customers in many ways, big and small. Even when you are seeking you are also giving. Questions you ask provide information about the research you have done, your body language provides cues as to your energy or interest in what is being said, and the list goes on. Just as you are always assessing the customer situation, customers are also assessing you.

Our focus on giving is the more formal process of providing or presenting information in the deployment of our sales tactics. There are dozens of books that provide detailed information on ways to organize and deliver a sales presentation. Here are some of our favorite tips on delivering a sales presentation:

- Take advantage of the natural spikes in listener attention in the beginning and end by organizing your points so that the most impactful are not in the middle when attention is lowest.

- To create "hooks" that enhance retention, use imagery, analogies, or number plays.

- Instead of words, when possible, use images on slides to illustrate your verbal communication.

## THE POWER OF STORIES IN SALES PRESENTATIONS

Our strongest suggestion is to use stories to execute the tactics focused on giving information. Stories have been shown to be the most effective ways to give information that can later be recalled. We have all grown up learning through stories, whether they are professionally produced books or movies, or tales specific to our families and communities. Stories are the oldest form of human communication, and they engage both the intellectual and emotional aspects of our brains.

Neurological studies have shown that information learned through stories is encoded differently in our brains than facts and figures.[2] We all know this: it is why we often create context when we attempt to memorize facts. The context is a story we are creating to hold the facts together. Stories are so powerful that often we create them when presented with conflicting or incomplete information. Many movies and novels are based upon the flawed story one character has created with partial or incomplete information. This may be entertaining to watch, but it is not what we want to happen during a sales cycle!

As salespeople, we can use stories to create a common, shared experience into which we invite our customers. If, for example, you have customers with a blind spot around the impact of their problems, explaining what they are missing will often lead to defensiveness, causing the customers to feel as if they are being "sold." However, sharing a story of another customer who had similar circumstances can open them up to reassessing their own situation.

The keys to a strong sales story are *relatability* and *specificity*. The story needs to be relatable to the new customers. And it must contain enough details so that the customers can feel like they are part of it without containing so many details that those details become distracting and the story becomes hard to follow.

---

> The keys to a strong sales story are *relatability* and
> *specificity*. The story needs to be relatable to
> the new customers. And it must contain enough details
> so that the customers can feel like they are part of it without
> containing so many details that those details become
> distracting and the story becomes hard to follow.

---

The type of story you share needs to reflect what you are trying to accomplish. There are three types of stories commonly used in sales, and each has a different intent (Table 11.1):

- *Solution stories* highlight the way your solution helped a customer with similar issues or concerns as the current

TABLE 11.1 **THREE TYPES OF STORIES COMMONLY USED IN SALES**

| Solution stories | Illustrate successful sales efforts |
|---|---|
| Foreshadowing stories | Highlight the consequences of inaction or poor decisions |
| Process stories | Share how your organization's processes improve the customer experience |

customer has. They detail how your product or service successfully addressed the customer's needs and the positive impact that resulted. Solution stories are often shared when deploying these tactics: *present solution* (consultative); *deliver your message* (competitive); *create awareness* (disruptive); and *clarify the ROI* (financial).

- *Foreshadowing stories* warn of the consequences of inaction. They describe what happened to customers who, when given the opportunity to make a brave choice, chose either the wrong action or inaction. The reasons why they avoided the brave choice (your solution) need to be relatable to your customer, as do the consequences of the poor choice. Foreshadowing stories are often successfully deployed in many of the same tactics as solution stories, especially if customers have shown some hesitancy or resistance. These stories are particularly valuable in the *disruptive strategy* because you are working with customers who may not see the impact of their current state.

- *Process stories* focus on the process for implementing a solution or supporting and enabling customers rather than the solution or product itself. Process stories can be very important when selling in an industry where there is minimal distinction between the actual products or services, and they can also be used anywhere a solution story is relevant. They are particularly useful if your organization's processes (implementation, payment, support, and so on) are differentiators. The disruptive tactic *coach the process* is focused on guiding customers in the steps they need to take to solve a previously unconsidered problem, and it is an obvious place for a process story.

Let's apply these story types to our fictional scenarios. A solution story may be very relevant in scenario 1. The customer is interested in comparing solutions, so having a strong example of how QuietTech's solutions helped a similar customer is a strong way to give information.

In scenario 2, both foreshadowing and process stories are strong choices. A foreshadowing story could be used to create awareness of what may happen if action is not taken. A process story could help make the process of addressing their noise issues relatable and ease any hesitation they may have about starting the process.

## SHARPENING YOUR STORYTELLING SKILLS FOR SALES STORIES

An Amazon search of "storytelling in business" yields over 3,000 results. Clearly, there are a lot of resources for those who want to sharpen their storytelling skills, and we are not attempting to compete with those experts. Our focus is on reinforcing that storytelling is an essential skill for sales agility.

We also want to emphasize that it is a skill most of us already possess to some degree and that improving it is a matter of focus and planning. It is tempting to think that the best stories are spontaneous, but that is rarely the case. A story meant to build rapport or create a connection can be done well in the moment. But sales stories, as we are describing them, are stories that are used to give information in support of a specific tactic. For these stories to be effective, salespeople need to adequately prepare. Crafting two or three stories that illustrate some of the common points you want to share within a sales cycle can help increase the agility with which you execute them.

## USING THE STORY ARC TO DEVELOP YOUR SALES STORY

To craft a strong story, we recommend following an amended version of the *story arc*, also known as a *narrative arc*. The story arc outlines the development of tension that gives a story shape. It begins with a *setting*, into which a *complication* is introduced, and tension begins to build. Tension continues as a *turning point* is reached; at which time the protagonist has a choice to make.

The right choice leads to a positive *resolution* and easing of tension. The wrong choice leads to further devolving into the circumstances created by the complication and ongoing tension. This is the story arc followed (loosely at times) by all stories (Figure 11.4). Think about any movie you know, and you will likely be able to pick out each of these elements.

For sales stories we suggest adding two elements to this arc. First, a clear reason *why* you are sharing the story: *Why* this story at this moment in the sales cycle? What are you trying to accomplish by sharing it? The story you craft should be clearly related to this *why*.

Second, you should add a *question* at the end of the story that invites the listeners to compare their situation to the one they just

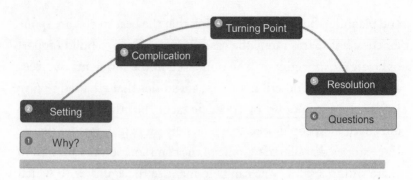

FIGURE 11.4  **The Story Arc**
*Source:* VantagePoint Performance.

heard about. For example, "What about that customer's situation feels similar to your own?" It is the question at the end of the story that transforms it into a powerful sales tool.

All sales tactics that are focused on giving information can benefit from the use of stories. In our first QuietTech scenario, we are deploying a *competitive* sales strategy, and we are focused on the *differentiate* sales tactic. As opposed to listing the features and benefits of your solution, it would be more impactful to share a story that highlighted a customer who weighed your solution against others and had a very specific reason, perhaps a feature or benefit, for choosing your solution.

In the second scenario, the early-stage opportunity, it may be best to share a story about how customers who, after wavering, decided to take their noise problems seriously. In each of these cases you are meeting the customers where they are and using stories to appeal to them both intellectually and emotionally.

We have one final point about stories and sales agility. The most agile sellers are very well versed in the art of sales storytelling. Why? Because using stories, when done correctly, makes selling easier. "Stories stick while facts fade." While we could not find the originator of this quote, the message is crystal clear. Too many salespeople rely on facts and figures to give customers the information they need to make an informed decision. This logic-based approach ignores the importance of emotion in the buying journey.

Agile sellers know that if they want customers to remember something, to be moved by it, they embed it in a story. If you want customers to share with others what they have learned from you, share a story that they find so compelling they want to share it. A story that resonates with your customers will take on a life of its own.

## SUMMARY

The third component of the Sales Agility Code, *execute*, is the focus of most sales training initiatives and programs. Understandably there is a lot of attention paid to the steps a salesperson takes to move an opportunity forward. Agile sellers are adept at executing the 12 tactics associated with the core sales strategies.

While each of these 12 tactics is focused on a specific sales task, they share common core skills: seeking information and giving information. Primary tools for seeking information are background, pain, and gain questions. *Background questions* ensure that you have context. *Pain questions* help define the negative impact of the status quo. *Gain questions* help clarify and broaden the positive consequences of change.

The most impactful way to give information is through *sales stories*. Three types of stories were introduced: *solution, foreshadowing*, and *process*. Stories create stronger recall and create an emotional connection to the information. The *story arc* is a proven way to create tension that draws in the listener and helps create a memorable story.

THE SALES AGILITY CODE

Agile salespeople make sales stories more impactful by adding two things to this arc. First, they *clarify* why they are telling that particular story at that moment in the buying journey, and second, they *ask* a prepared follow-up question that invites the customers to personalize what they just heard.

## KEY TAKEAWAYS

- *Choosing* and *executing* are what agile sellers do once they have assessed a buyer's situation.

- *Choosing* requires both strategic and tactical decisions. Strategically, sellers answer the question, What sales path is best aligned with the customers' buying situation?

- FSU found and VantagePoint validated that each sales strategy had three tactics most aligned with it. That alignment, however, was fluid, and any tactic could potentially be used with any strategy.

- Sellers are *executing* when they deploy the chosen tactic in support of the chosen strategy.

- The 12 sales tactics share two foundational execution skills: seeking information and giving information.

- Stories are the most impactful way to give information in a sales process. Stories engage both the emotional and rational mind, and they are easier for buyers to recall. There are three types of sales stories described: *solution*, *foreshadowing*, and *process*.

# PART V

# THE PATH TO
# SALES EXPERTISE

CHAPTER **12**

# Coaching Sales Agility

What comes to mind when you hear the word *coaching*? Perhaps your first thought is athletics. Or maybe you think of your annual performance review or a pipeline review. *Coaching* is a term that is used broadly, and often inappropriately. One organization we work with uses the term "coach them out" to indicate that coaching is the mechanism used to convince poor performers to quit. You can imagine that employees are not lining up for coaching in that organization!

Most of the coaching initiatives offered in medium to large businesses are focused on general developmental coaching. Few focus on sales coaching specifically. This is a problem because coaching a salesperson is not the same as coaching an accountant or an engineer. The nature of a sales job is substantially different. Salespeople are focused on revenue acquisition or growth. Their job is not bound by a task, project, or assignment with a (mostly) clear path forward. Their job is to influence other people to change their behavior. Their job is to be agile.

In this chapter, we will not attempt to cover all that could be covered on this topic—there are hundreds of books that try to do that. Our focus in this chapter is exclusively on sales coaching, and more precisely, on sales agility coaching. VantagePoint's research has revealed the management practices of high-performing sales managers. This research is described in our book *Crushing Quota: Proven Sales Coaching Tactics for Breakthrough Performance*. We will touch on only a few of the most relevant findings here as they relate to coaching agility.

Sales agility coaching can be defined as equipping salespeople to perform a high-impact activity consistently well. The specific activity varies depending on what you are focused on: organizational, situational, or foundational agility. We will address tips related to each of these areas of focus later in this chapter. First, let's focus on what VantagePoint's research found that characterizes the most effective sales coaching conversations.

## PLANNING FOR SALES COACHING

Sales coaching that is planned and scheduled is often more impactful than spontaneous, in-the-moment coaching. You may be thinking, "Wait! You want me to plan coaching on agility?" It does sound a bit odd, but it is what we are saying. Think about professional sports teams that have planned practices and planned scrimmages even though game-time execution is primarily agile.

In-the-moment coaching serves an important purpose, and we're not suggesting omitting it from a coaching repertoire. However, VantagePoint's research showed that spontaneous coaching conversations are not the most effective way to influence performance. The most impactful coaching is planned to meet a specific purpose—supporting seller execution of a specific sales activity. When coaching agility, that purpose would be to enhance the execution of a sales activity such as assessing a buyer's situation or executing a disruptive strategy.

> The most impactful coaching is planned to
> meet a specific purpose—supporting seller
> execution of a specific sales activity.

Planning allows you to proactively identify what to coach so that both the sales manager and the salesperson can be prepared and ready to fully participate in the conversation. This is not as cumbersome as it may sound. Planning requires identifying just three things:

1. *Input:* The preparation activities that ensure that both the salesperson and manager are fully prepared to engage in the coaching discussion

2. *Agenda:* The focus of your coaching

3. *Output:* The anticipated outcome of the conversation

For example, a coaching plan focused on a sellers' ability to choose a sales strategy based on their assessment of the customer situation may look like this:

**Inputs**

- Seller provides the sales manager the names of three active opportunities to discuss in the coaching session.

- The seller is prepared to discuss how their choice of sales strategy reflects their assessment of the buyer situation and which tactic they plan to deploy and why.

- Manager reviews account notes in the customer relationship management (CRM) system prior to meeting.

**Agenda**

- Update on opportunities discussed in the last meeting. What went well? Surprises?

- For each opportunity shared as input:
  - Review the seller's assessment of the current buying situation.
    - > What evidence contributed to their conclusions?
  - Discuss the choice of sales strategy.
    - > How was the choice made?
  - Discuss the choice of sales tactic.
    - > Which sales tactic is most critical for this opportunity at this stage? Why?
  - Agree to next steps.

**Output**

- Distribute updated opportunity notes and/or plans in the CRM per agreements.

A plan such as the one above makes a sales manager's life easier and provides significant value to the seller. Since the plan is specific to opportunity coaching and not to a specific seller, it can be used repeatedly and with each salesperson on the team.

Knowing exactly what will be discussed allows both the manager and seller to prepare fully and gives the manager permission to lean on the seller for contributions to the conversation. It also encourages deep conversation about specific activity execution as opposed to a surface review of general execution. Vantage-Point's research is clear that spending more time coaching fewer opportunities in depth was more impactful than covering many opportunities lightly.

## HOW TO CONDUCT COACHING CONVERSATIONS

Even the best coaching plan relies on the sales manager to bring it to life through an interactive and collaborative conversation. Not surprisingly, the best sales coaching conversations are like the best sales conversations. They both have a clear purpose, they are focused on the customer or seller being coached, and they end with a clear next step. And, as in an effective sales call, the less the manager shares when coaching, the more they can elicit meaningful input from the salesperson.

So, it's not surprising that VantagePoint's *coaching conversation model* reflects a similar approach to the best sales conversations. Figure 12.1 illustrates the flow of the coaching conversation, highlighting the importance of give-and-take between a manager and a salesperson.

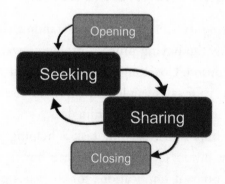

FIGURE 12.1 **Coaching Conversation Model**
*Source:* VantagePoint Performance.

Effective coaching conversations begin with the *opening*, during which the manager creates a comfortable environment and clearly expresses and gains agreement on the purpose of the conversation.

The opening flows into the heart of the coaching conversation: the interplay between *seeking* and *giving* information.

*Seeking* is when the manager uncovers the salesperson's ideas and challenges and solicits ideas for future execution. *Giving* is when the manager shares insights, perspectives, and ideas to help the salesperson maximize their effectiveness, overcome their challenges, or think about something in a different way. Seeking and giving iterate throughout the coaching conversation.

*Closing* is an important final step, just as it is in a sales conversation. A strong close ensures that there is clarity on next steps and accountability for completing them. Ideally, a manager prompts the salesperson to summarize the next steps so that there is no doubt that they understand what has been discussed. The flow of the coaching conversation model is consistent across topics; however, *what* you focus on depends on which *activity and associated skills* you are targeting.

## COACHING FOUNDATIONAL AGILITY

*Foundational agility* is focused on understanding three buying situation factors: the buying process, problem awareness, and the solution definition. Coaching foundational agility is focused on ensuring that your salespeople know how to assess these factors and align their selling efforts accordingly.

The first important coaching task is helping the salesperson determine the buyers' location within their buying journey as that will have significant implications for the sales process (Figure 12.2). There are two key areas of focus that coaching foundational agility should address:

- *The buying journey:* Where are these buyers in their journey? Are they at identify needs, establish criteria, assess solutions, or mitigate risk? What is the evidence for this determination?

- *Planning for sales conversations:* What are the buyers' likely motivators and objectives for a next meeting based on which buying stage they're in?

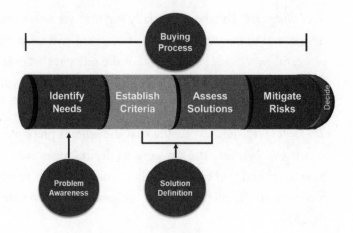

FIGURE 12.2 **The Buying Journey**
*Source:* VantagePoint Performance.

## Coaching Aligned to the Buying Journey

Each stage of the buying journey requires a shift in focus for the seller and a corresponding shift in the focus of coaching conversations. The focus of coaching should support the seller's primary task given the buyer's current situation.

### Identify Needs

*The selling task:* To gather information about the buyers' current situation, uncover and expand any problems or pain the buyer is experiencing, and determine the degree to which the buyers would like to solve their problems.

207

*The focus of coaching:* To verify the seller's ability to conduct research, ask *pain questions*, expand pain awareness, share stories from other customers, or express appropriate empathy.

### Establish Criteria

*The selling task:* To take potentially vague buyer needs and desires and shape them into specific buying criteria using powerful *gain questions.* The goal of the seller at this point is to shape the buying criteria in such a way as to allow the seller to best position and differentiate their solutions.

*The focus of coaching:* To ensure that the seller is prepared to ask *gain questions* and can convert desires uncovered to buying criteria that favor the seller's solution. Also, to obtain buy-in from the customers that those buying criteria are priorities.

### Assess Solutions

*The selling task:* To offer your solution as the best fit to the buyers' criteria. The seller needs to make it very clear that their solution meets the buying criteria better than competing alternatives.

*The focus of coaching:* To ensure that the seller can communicate the solution fit engagingly, which may involve storytelling, presentation techniques, or obtaining commitment.

### Mitigate Risk

*The selling task:* To provide proof points to the buyers to alleviate any concerns and increase buyer confidence in the seller's solution.

*The focus of coaching:* To ensure that the seller has proof points that will resonate with the buyers and to focus on listening skills, expressing empathy, problem solving, or storytelling.

Once the buyers' location within their buying journey has been determined and their likely objectives identified, other relevant buying factors come into play. For example, if the buyers are in the *identify needs* stage of their buying journey, it is highly likely that *problem awareness* is a primary topic of interest to them. Alternatively, if the buyers are in either the *establish criteria* or *assess solutions* stage, then the *solution definition* is highly relevant. The reason we care about where the buyers are within their buying journey is because that initial determination sets the trajectory for the choices sellers make and how they execute those choices.

## Coaching the Seller's Plan for Sales Conversations

The next task is to help the salesperson plan their upcoming sales conversation. The focus of coaching here is ensuring that the seller appropriately aligns their sales objective to the buyers' journey. Sellers should always align to the buyers, not the other way around. This is critical because it is almost impossible to influence buyers if the buyers don't feel understood.

### Identify Needs

*The selling task:* To anticipate buyer problems and consequences of these problems. This is the heart of problem awareness.

*The focus of coaching:* To help the seller see the world through the buyers' lens, anticipating aspects of the buyers' environment and challenges. This will help prepare the seller to effectively qualify the viability of an opportunity. If no serious pain exists, it is unlikely the buyers will be motivated to make a change. Buyers are twice as likely to act to avoid pain than to achieve gain—so helping the seller empathetically dig into buyer pain is a high-impact skill.

## Establish Criteria

*The selling task:* To shape buyer needs into specific buying criteria that align closely with the seller's solutions.

*The focus of coaching:* To ensure that the seller does not rely on assumptions. Often sellers believe that their thinking and the buyers' thinking are aligned when it actually is not. The more specific the buying criteria are, the easier it is for sellers to differentiate their solutions. Buyers like their own ideas better than ours. Their problems, needs, and associated buying criteria must be acknowledged by the buyers, in the buyers' own words, to be valid.

## Assess Solutions

*The selling task:* To offer solutions in an engaging and easy-to-consume manner that resonates with the buyers and to differentiate solutions from competitors.

*The focus of coaching:* To prepare the seller to offer solutions aligned to the buying criteria, as well as to differentiate them from competing alternatives. Buyers are no longer satisfied to learn about sellers' solutions in a vacuum. They want sellers to help them make sense of the solutions they're considering, understand the potential trade-offs, and narrow the scope of the decision.

## Mitigate Risk

*The selling task:* To understand buyer concerns, the reasons for those concerns, as well as the best ways to effectively mitigate the risks buyers feel in making a purchase decision.

*The focus of coaching:* To help the sellers anticipate the buyers' concerns and perceived risks and increase their confidence to proactively address these concerns before a sale stalls. Buyers want to avoid making a mistake. They want to minimize or eliminate buyer's remorse. Sellers who don't anticipate this stage often get worried that the deal is falling apart. They have less contact with the buyers, and they begin to think the worst. Coaching should help sellers understand that this risk-aversion dynamic on the part of the buyers is a very natural part of the selling process.

# WHY COACHING FOUNDATIONAL AGILITY MATTERS

The number one cause of stalled deals in any seller's pipeline is poor qualification. Many sellers get overly optimistic about the viability of the deals they are pursuing. They look for buying signals, and when they hear them, they are off to the races. Managers who orient a healthy portion of their opportunity and sales call coaching to the early stages of the sales cycles outperform managers who focus primarily on the later stages.

Deals that are improperly qualified and/or poorly shaped are harder to win. Managers who wait until deals are in the *assess solutions* or *mitigate risk* stages are at a distinct disadvantage. Deals in the late stages are often very well shaped, and oftentimes not by the sellers being coached. This creates the need for sales manager heroics, which are unnatural acts by the sales managers to win poorly qualified deals.

Deep discounting and heavy negotiation are often a result of deals that are not well qualified, where the buyers feel very little urgency to make a change. The customers' problem awareness and their unique solution definitions are the key ingredients that drive clarity and motivate them to act.

Helping sellers attend to the buying journey, problem awareness, and solution definition will result in more winnable deals and healthier pipelines. It also warrants mentioning that helping sellers plan for upcoming sales calls is far more powerful than observing and debriefing calls that the sales manager did not help plan.

## COACHING SITUATIONAL AGILITY

*Situational agility* expands on foundational agility. It relies on a comprehensive assessment of the buyers' situation, a well-considered choice of a sales strategy, and a strong execution of sales tactics in support of that strategy. Each of these three components—assess, choose, and execute—provides specific coaching opportunities.

Situational agility also relies on an agility mindset. This mindset is characterized by curiosity, objectivity, and a customer-first orientation. The agility mindset is also rich fodder for coaching conversations and best addressed through the application of activities related to assess, choose, and execute.

### Coaching the Sellers' Ability to Assess

*The selling task:* To seek and orient relevant information on the customers' situation, ensuring the consideration of a wide range of buying factors while doing so.

*The focus of coaching:* To ensure that sellers are assessing as fully and objectively as possible. There are three areas on which to focus this coaching. First, coaches must ensure that sellers are considering all aspects of the situation before jumping into choose or execute. Often salespeople stop assessing after hearing some type of buying signal. Coaching salespeople to pause and seek more deeply is critical. The five categories of buying situation factors can be a useful coaching tool here (Figure 12.3). Are there certain factors that a seller tends to overlook or minimize? Are there factors that are tightly aligned to situations in which you are most successful?

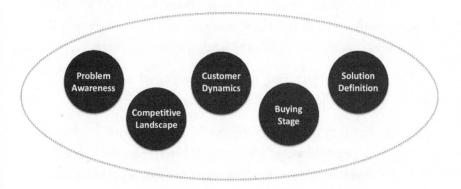

FIGURE 12.3 **The Buying Situation Factors Categories**
*Source:* VantagePoint Performance.

Second, coaches must help sellers strengthen *how* their sellers approach the assess step of their decision-making framework. Are they overly reliant on one of the four methods of seeking: conversation, observation, research, or feedback? How strong are they at executing each of those methodologies? For example, are they able to ask questions that are both valuable to the customers and helpful in gathering useful information? Do they have numerous sources for researching the customers or the industry? Do they pick up on feedback that is impactful to understanding shifts in the situation?

Third, and perhaps most challenging, coaches must support the sellers' ability to make sense of, or orient, the information they have gathered to create a comprehensive picture of the customer situation. The sellers must be able to apply a perspective to the information gathered and determine how it all fits together, without letting their own biases affect what they are seeing. In other words, they need to determine which aspects of the buying situation combine to create a relevant and accurate picture and which factors may be just noise. Coaching the ability to orient focuses on asking sellers to share and explain the decisions they have made.

Assess is often the area that requires the most coaching. Staying objective is hard. To help your salespeople improve their ability to assess, consider the following as you prepare to coach:

- Are they gathering as much information as is reasonable given where they are in the sales cycle?

- Are they remaining objective? As stated above, salespeople (consciously or not) listen for certain clues that link to a solution they can offer. Some of that is inevitable, but it can minimize how deeply they seek and result in surprises that derail the sale.

- Are they orienting—that is, are they making sense of what they've learned? Not all information is equal in terms of its relevance to a customer situation. Are salespeople focusing on the most important aspects, or are they distracted by less relevant information?

Coaching the ability to assess is the most important situational agility coaching task. If sellers do not assess well, every other decision they make is compromised.

## Coaching the Sellers' Ability to Choose

*The selling task:* Identifying the sales approach or strategy that will most likely be successful given the buyers' situation and choosing the optimal sales tactics to execute in support of that strategy.

*Focus of coaching:* To identify how sellers make their choices. Which strategy have they decided is the best path to winning this opportunity? Which of the 12 tactics have they decided is the next best step to accomplishing that? As we have discussed, salespeople often have overdeveloped muscles in the strategies they were trained to use. The coach's most important role is to ensure that the sellers are making a conscious choice based on an alignment to the customer situation, *not* comfort level, with a sales approach.

Digging into the reasons for their choice, to ensure that it is well grounded in what was identified in *assess* is the primary coaching focus here. The coach's job is not to look for the right choice but rather to understand how the salespeople made their decisions. Why those specific tactics? How do they see it playing out? Of course, choosing an impactful sales strategy is only possible if the assessment of the situation was strong. Often *assess* and *choose* are coached together.

## Coaching Sellers' Ability to Execute

*The selling task:* To execute the specific sales tactic chosen in pursuit of advancing the opportunity.

*The focus of coaching:* To support execution of the tactic by ensuring that the sellers are prepared. The execution of specific sales tactics is the most common focus of sales coaching, and there are many ways sales managers can add value. The specific coaching focus varies based on the tactic chosen, but it is always some combination of seeking information from the customers or sharing information with them.

In general terms, the best focus here is on how the sellers are *planning* to use the specific strategy: What questions will they be asking and why? How will they be sharing or presenting information? This is not the way it is always done. Often coaching happens only retroactively, after customer interactions: "Let's discuss what worked and what did not." Those discussions are valuable, but they become more valuable when preceded by coaching on what the sellers are planning to do, digging into the why and the how. Having a strong plan provides a secure basis upon which to execute agility when needed.

Coaching how sellers plan to execute gives coaches a chance to pressure test their logic as well as the actual execution of the specific tactic. For example, if a seller is planning to execute *create awareness*, a tactic within the *disruptive strategy*, the coach could investigate what information the seller is planning on sharing to disrupt the customer assumptions as well as having the salesperson practice delivering that information.

---

**Coaching how sellers plan to execute gives coaches a chance to pressure test their logic as well as the actual execution of the specific tactic.**

---

In Chapter 11, we presented two core skills that are shared by all sales tactics: *seeking information* and *giving information*. When coaching a tactic that relies on *seeking* information, consider how well your salesperson does the following:

- Asks a broad variety of open-ended questions that provide value to the customer

- Asks second- or third-level questions to dig into information shared

- Taps into customer motives by asking pain and gain questions

- Plans questions appropriate to the sales tactic and current buying situation

When coaching a tactic that relies on *giving* information, consider how well your salesperson does the following:

- Chooses stories that will resonate with the specific customer

- Helps the customer connect to the story by including enough (but not too much) background information

- Includes challenges the specific customer is currently facing

- Highlights the role the customer in the story played in ensuring a positive resolution or, conversely, how they missed the opportunity to save the day

- Asks strong open-ended questions after the story to encourage the customer to share how it relates to their situation

- Shares the story in an engaging manner

# FEEDBACK

The ability to perceive and incorporate new information is a core attribute of agility in any field. *Feedback* is essential to the agile execution of the other three components: *assess*, *choose*, and *execute*.

The most agile salespeople are always alert to new information that may affect or even dramatically change the decisions made in *assess*, *choose*, and *execute*. Feedback can happen at any point and is therefore not typically coached on its own. That does not mean, however, that it doesn't deserve specific attention from sales managers as part of ongoing coaching conversations.

## Coaching on Sellers' Ability to Process Feedback

*The selling task:* To seek feedback in multiple ways, make sense of what is gathered, and incorporate relevant information to revise previous decisions and determine new ones.

*The focus of coaching:* To help sellers gather, understand, and incorporate new information into their decisions. The most obvious sources of feedback are the customers. Their reaction to something the sellers did or a change in their internal planning can dramatically alter the picture of the customer situation. Feedback can also come from industry news or a new competitor entering the field. Feedback sometimes comes in the form of an absence of something.

We have all had customers who have "gone silent" or never followed through on commitments. That silence is important feedback to build into decision-making. Sales managers coach their sellers on how attuned they are to feedback, how they incorporate that feedback into their current thinking, and how open they are to changing direction to stay aligned to the new situation.

## COACHING ORGANIZATIONAL AGILITY

Coaching organizational agility involves making three distinct, yet interrelated decisions about sales execution. First, sales managers must align salesperson activity with organizational goals and marketplace realities. Second, sales managers must orient sales coaching to those seller activities that matter most. Finally, sales managers must attend to leading indicators of progress to determine if the right metrics are moving in the right direction. These three decisions and associated actions form the basis of effective ongoing sales management and coaching.

VantagePoint has done extensive research on how to best align sales activities to organizational results (Figure 12.4). Our findings are detailed in our books, *Crushing Quota* and *Cracking the Sales Management Code*. In brief, identifying these sale activities requires three steps:

- First, figure out which business results you're targeting.

- Second, determine which sales objectives are necessary to achieve those results.

- And finally, decide what sales activities must be executed consistently well to achieve those results. Which sales activities will have the highest impact?

Coaching the identified high-impact activities is done in much the same way foundational and situational agility is coached. In fact, there is often overlap between the high-impact activity and either situational or foundational agility. For example, call planning

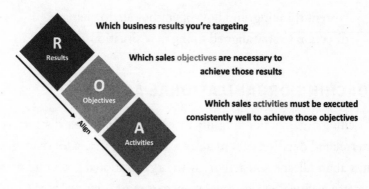

Which business results you're targeting

Which sales objectives are necessary to
achieve those results

Which sales activities must be executed
consistently well to achieve those objectives

FIGURE 12.4 **Aligning Organizational Results to Sales Activities**
*Source:* VantagePoint Performance.

is often a high-impact activity related to affecting certain KPIs
such as expanding share of wallet.

While focusing on the call planning being done for a specific
opportunity at a specific buying stage, managers are also looking
at the skill of call planning: Are they including the right elements
in the plan? Are they organizing the call well? Coaching organizational agility includes activities relevant to foundational and situational agility, but also includes others such as mining territories
or retaining existing accounts.

## SUMMARY

Sales coaching is distinctly different from general developmental coaching. It is growth focused and more open-ended than
other, less variable types of jobs such as accounting or finance.
This is one of the primary reasons that general leadership coaching
doesn't translate well to sales coaching. Coaching is a very broad
topic, and it was not covered exhaustively in this chapter. Instead,
we narrowed our focus to the specifics involved in coaching agility.

The most effective sales coaching is formally structured and
scheduled, and it involves covering fewer topics in greater depth.

Good sales coaching is highly collaborative, involving a good balance of seeking and giving. The most impactful coaching is planned to meet a specific purpose—that is, it supports seller execution of a specific sales activity. Coaching conversations that focus on planning upcoming sales conversations are more powerful than debriefs of past sales conversations.

Coaching foundational sales agility is focused on the *buyers' journey*, *problem awareness*, and *solution definition*. The content of foundational agility coaching should relate directly to the buyers' position within their buying journey. Coaching situational agility expands the scope of assessment to additional factors of the buying situation, including *customer dynamics* and *competitive landscape*.

The most challenging aspect of situational agility coaching is ensuring that the sellers properly assess and make sense of the buying situation the sellers are facing. Coaching strategy and tactic choice and proper execution is also a vital part of coaching situational agility. Coaching organizational agility involves ensuring frontline sales execution aligns with organizational goals and marketplace realities.

## KEY TAKEAWAYS

- Sales coaching discussions should include the following:
  - Inputs or preparation activities for manager and seller
  - Agendas to drive the focus of the coaching
  - Outputs or agreed-upon next steps
- The best coaching conversations are highly collaborative with a balance of giving and seeking behaviors.
- Coaching foundational agility starts with the establishment of where the buyers are within their buying journey: *identify needs*, *establish criteria*, *assess solutions*, or *mitigate risk*.

- Coaching sellers to plan for upcoming sales conversations is more powerful than debriefing conversations after they've happened.

- Coaching situational agility involves a deeper assessment of the buying situation, including these aspects:
    - Problem awareness
    - Competitive landscape
    - Customer dynamics
    - Buying stage
    - Solution definition

- Coaching organizational agility involves these elements:
    - Selecting and executing the most important activities sellers must execute in order to accomplish organizational goals
    - Formalizing and structuring coaching conversations around the highest-impact activities
    - Assessing leading indicators of progress, and making adjustments as needed

## CHAPTER 13

# How Salespeople Become Experts

Have you ever wondered why your ability to play golf or tennis has plateaued even though you play every week? Have you ever wondered why some people continue to improve while others stagnate? Is it natural talent, or some inherent trait that makes them better? It is common to find recreational golfers, tennis players, and skiers who have not improved their performance after years, or even decades, of regular experience.

There is a common assumption that the more you do something, the better you get at it. Yet studies by K. Anders Ericsson have shown that there is almost no correlation between experience and expertise.[1] Similarly, after the first year of execution, there is only a weak correlation between performance and length of experience after individuals have gained their initial experience.

Studies by K. Anders Ericsson have shown that there is almost no correlation between experience and expertise.[2]

Dr. Ericsson studied expertise more than any other researcher, and he made some interesting discoveries.[3] Ericsson dispelled the notion that natural athleticism or superior intelligence are required for expert performance. This position is in direct contrast with common sense. Most of us think that the best athletes are just more athletic. The best musicians are just more naturally gifted. The best salespeople are just naturally gregarious.

While athleticism, personality traits, and being gifted may be helpful, they are not the true source of expertise. So how do experts achieve what some of us do not? In this chapter we explore the topic of expertise and how it is best attained in a sales context. Specifically, we differentiate between different levels of skills, how we approach acquiring those skills, the traps we encounter, and the extra steps experts take that lead to expert performance.

## THE DIFFERENCE BETWEEN AMATEURS AND EXPERTS

When we are learning a new skill or sport, the early stages of learning consist of avoiding mistakes. We are actively trying to reduce mistakes, and we often improve rapidly. As we gain experience, we make fewer mistakes. This makes sense. At this point, learning no longer focuses on achieving what we consider an acceptable level of performance. The tasks, like golf, tennis, and even selling, become automated or habitual, and we stop thinking so much about them. Anyone who has been driving for more than a week knows this is true. Once a task has become automated, more experience does not typically lead to better performance. This explains why there is a very low correlation between experience and expertise over time.

Getting better at a task—whether it is golf, tennis, or selling—requires practice that takes individuals beyond their current comfort zone and challenges them to improve performance. Figure 13.1 shows the difference in expertise gained over time for different types of tasks.

FIGURE 13.1  **Experience and Expert Performance**

*Source:* Adapted from K. Anders Ericsson, "The Influence of Experience and Deliberate Practice on the Development of Superior Expert Performance," in *Generalizable Mechanisms Mediating Expertise and General Issues*, edited by K. Anders Ericsson, Neil Charness, Paul J. Feltovich, and Robert F. Hoffman (Cambridge, UK: Cambridge University Press, 2006), doi: https://doi.org/10.1017/CBO9780511816796.038.

Simple tasks like brushing your teeth, cooking eggs, and making your bed are all about habituation. Since the tasks are not complex, they become second nature, operating below conscious awareness. Even more complex tasks like driving become habituated over time. We suddenly realize that we've reached our destination, yet barely remember the drive. This doesn't mean that we weren't paying attention. We were. Just not dedicated, highly conscious attention.

When we graduate to tasks like golf, tennis, and other recreational sports, our initial attention is very focused. We aim to improve performance through practice until we reach an acceptable level. Once we reach what we consider an acceptable level, we shift away from improvement, and instead focus on getting enjoyment from playing. This acceptable level of performance is where we often stop our growth. This ceasing of continued improvement is called *arrested development*.

You might be wondering what golf has to do with sales. Well, for many of us the dynamics at play in golf reflect similar dynamics at play in selling. Once we've gained an acceptable level of expertise in selling, we think we've arrived. We've punched the ticket and gotten the T-shirt. Or so we think. What we don't realize is that we still have room for growth, room to get better. We confuse experience with expertise, settling for a performance level that is acceptable, yet not necessarily desirable.

So, if experience does not create sales expertise, what does? What do sellers do that allows them to move past novice to expert? According to Ericsson, experts engage in deliberate practice. They practice in a way that inherently leads to better performance. They practice highly specific tasks related to their domain in a very deliberate way.

As you see in Figure 13.2, deliberate practice incorporates four primary elements:

1. *A clear and specific goal:* The task at hand must be bounded and clearly defined.

2. *Focus on that goal:* Perform the task.

3. *Feedback:* Individuals must obtain feedback on the effectiveness of the task.

4. *A push beyond the comfort zone:* This is where the feedback introduces additional complexity to the task to take the individual to a higher level of skill.

FIGURE 13.2  **Four Components of Deliberate Practice**

*Source:* Adapted from K. Anders Ericsson, "The Influence of Experience and Deliberate Practice on the Development of Superior Expert Performance," in *Generalizable Mechanisms Mediating Expertise and General Issues*, edited by K. Anders Ericsson, Neil Charness, Paul J. Feltovich, and Robert F. Hoffman (Cambridge, UK: Cambridge University Press, 2006), doi: https://doi.org/10.1017/CBO9780511816796.038.

---

Experts engage in deliberate practice. They practice in a way that inherently leads to better performance.

---

## THE ROLE OF COACHES AND TEACHERS IN DEVELOPING EXPERTISE

In addition, no individual reaches elite status without the help of coaches and teachers. Those coaches and teachers help structure practice to ensure consistent improvement through continuously increased challenges. This method of deliberate practice raises the performance beyond its current level. Some common methods of deliberate practice include role playing.

Let's look at a simple sales example to see how deliberate practice works. Let's assume the sales manager is helping the seller prepare for an important upcoming sales conversation. The seller is worried about a specific objection and is not confident in her ability to handle it effectively:

*Potential objection:* Your product is relatively new to market. I'm worried that your product has not been properly vetted and tested compared to your competitors' products. Theirs have been around for much longer.

*Seller response:* We have a very extensive testing process. We do alpha and beta tests with both customers and labs for 24 months prior to a product launch. Our vetting and testing process is one of the most comprehensive in the industry.

*Feedback from sales manager:* Well, you are certainly correct about our vetting and testing process. It is one of the most robust in our industry. When you've provided this response in the past, how have customers reacted?

*Seller:* They have believed that we have a robust process, but it hasn't seemed to satisfy them. I've given them white papers of our testing process, and they still don't feel comfortable. They feel the competitors are better proven and established.

*Sales manager:* Why are our products newer in the market?

*Seller:* Because we have better innovations. Our research has led to new capabilities that the competing products don't have. That's why they haven't been around as long.

*Sales manager:* So, what would happen if before responding, you tested the buyers' level of interest in newer innovations. Specifically, how would the new capabilities improve throughput and productivity in the lab?

*Seller:* So, what if I said something like this: "I agree that our products have not been around as long as our competitors'. One of the reasons for that is because our research and development have led to new innovations with this specific type of product. When you think about your lab and some of the challenges your lab techs face, how important is it for them to have the most current technology to ensure more accurate testing and faster results?"

*Sales manager:* Let's try that out. I'll be the lab manager. Let's role-play this objection using your most recent idea.

Although coaching is an integral part of deliberate practice, feedback isn't always delivered in a way that *mirrors* deliberate practice. Take a typical sales call debrief. The sales manager takes notes of what the salesperson did well and identifies areas of improvement. Agreements are made. End of story. What's missing from this typical feedback approach is the last piece of the puzzle: pushing beyond the comfort zone.

Suppose the sales call debrief discussion were to continue and the sales manager asked, "When you asked that question about ... and the customer responded with . . . , what additional questions could you have asked to test his level of buy-in?" This would elevate the manager's feedback and coaching in a way that reflects deliberate practice. This augmented approach takes the effectiveness of coaching to a much higher level, one that promotes acquisition of expertise. In this example, it's simply a function of the sales manager asking a different and deeper question to force reflection and drive critical thinking.

In addition to live coaching, there are alternative ways of achieving deliberate practice. Salespeople and sales managers can be presented with increasingly challenging scenarios to determine how well they respond to them. Immediate feedback can be given, and the seller (or sales manager) can redo the task incorporating the feedback. This can be done asynchronously and incorporate the components of deliberate practice as indicated in Figure 13.2. This approach can amplify the impact of deliberate practice since it is scalable across a sales organization. Furthermore, it contributes to the core elements of sales agility: better critical thinking and decision-making.

## EXPERT SALES MANAGERS AND SALESPEOPLE ARE BETTER DECISION MAKERS

According to Ericsson, expert performers have acquired mental models that allow them to access relevant information that supports flexible reasoning about a task or situation. This advantage that experts exhibit is about anticipatory skills rather than innate abilities. They know what to look for, and they know what to do when they find it. It is about equipping oneself with a decision-making model to internally monitor what is happening and compare it with the goal. This internal monitoring is highly task specific. These decision-making mechanisms displayed by experts allow them to transcend the limiting factors present in an amateur's performance and avoid the arrested development associated with automated tasks.

Recent research indicates that high-performing sales managers and salespeople are better decision makers and that the high quality of their decisions leads to better performance. How does this work? Well, let's start with sales managers.

Our management practices research, published in our book *Crushing Quota*, indicates that high-performing managers do not just do more than their lower-performing peers. They do things differently. They coach fewer hours, for longer durations, and discuss fewer topics. What do they coach? The activities that are most critical for achievement of their KPIs and associated quotas. They are maniacal about prioritizing what matters most and attending to those priorities in very structured, effective ways. These managers make better decisions about *what* to coach and *how* to coach. The better decision-making ultimately leads to better coaching and better coaching outcomes. But what about salespeople?

---

**High-performing managers do not just do more than their lower-performing peers. They do things differently.**

---

Research into the way high-performing sellers work (originally conducted by Florida State University's Sales Institute and expanded by VantagePoint) found that high-performing sellers were agile. They adjusted their sales approach based on the buying situation they faced. In other words, they evaluated the situation they were facing and chose the optimal path forward. They didn't use a one-size-fits-all approach. High-performing sellers spent more time than average sellers assessing their buying situations *prior* to selecting and executing an appropriate sales strategy. They also were more likely to vet their ideas with a respected peer or their sales manager to test the quality of their thinking. It was the high quality of these assessments and decisions that led to better execution and better outcomes.

## IMPLICATIONS FOR SALES ENABLEMENT

Effective sales enablement involves (1) identifying which behaviors lead to the highest performance, (2) structuring training activities around those behaviors, (3) monitoring trainee performance against standards, and (4) providing increasingly challenging practice and feedback over time as performance improves. This implies a long-term approach to sales enablement compared with the more traditional episodic approach to training. For this reason, most of our clients realize the need for more robust enablement over time, and they choose to engage with us for multiple years. Developing expertise in sports and in selling is an ongoing endeavor. Maintaining expertise requires continuing practice, feedback, and coaching.

If we consider the research findings for high-performing sales managers and salespeople, we can tie their behavior to deliberate practice that can be implemented within the sales enablement function. Sales managers can be trained in ways that educate sellers on better decision-making that replicates high-performer behavior in assessing the situations the sellers are facing (which seller, in which situation); on selecting the best type of coaching (which high-impact activity to coach, within which frequency, duration, and topics); and then on applying that coaching rhythm over time.

Salespeople can be trained to identify the buying factors that most significantly affect their buyers, to determine how those factors align into unique buying situations, and then to choose and execute the best sales strategy that will lead to a win. These decision-making frameworks for both salespeople and sales managers represent Ericsson's point about mental models used by experts to improve their analysis and decision-making.

This development framework stands in sharp contrast to the way most salespeople and sales managers are trained. Most sellers are trained in an individual methodology and instructed to use that approach in every buying situation. Most sales managers are taught a step-by-step coaching model to apply to all their coaching efforts. These procedural approaches take the decision-making, and overall effectiveness, out of many enablement efforts.

## THE ROLE OF REFLECTION
## AND POSTMORTEMS AS A PATH
## TO IMPROVEMENT

VantagePoint research has consistently indicated that the highest-performing sales managers conduct postmortems of wins and losses. These postmortems allow managers and sellers to thoroughly explore the sequence of events of a deal to identify strengths and areas for improvement. One major impediment to conducting effective postmortems is the lack of the customers' commitment to conducting them.

A way around this is to ask the customers very early in the sales process if they would be willing to do a debrief whether the opportunity is won or lost. Early in the buying journey, it is highly unlikely that customers will refuse this request. Very late in the buying journey, customers are less willing to spend the time, particularly with vendors who did not make the final cut or win the deal. Setting yourself up for a successful postmortem is about establishing expectations and gaining agreement very early in the process.

The most effective postmortems examine a few key topics for losses and wins that can be asked to both seller and buyer. The questions we offer here are by no means an exhaustive list, but they have been designed to help you gain vital information about your effectiveness at helping buyers navigate their journey and to help you write your own list. In this environment of overinformed customers and intense competition, we can never rest on our laurels and assume that we've done everything right. In fact, assumptions are the primary cause of lost deals. When we take the time to understand the dynamics of each sale, we take that intelligence into every future sale. This additional step in the sales process ensures

In fact, assumptions are the primary cause of lost deals.
When we take the time to understand the dynamics of each
sale, we take that intelligence into every future sale.

that sellers gain true expertise, rather than simply compiling additional experience:

## Losses

- Who were the relevant competitors?

- What specific relevant differentiators did the winner possess that we didn't?

- Where did we fall short in the ratings of all included vendors?

- Which client needs and priorities were critical to this deal?

- How did we align with those needs and priorities?

- What was the primary messaging and positioning that resonated with the customer, both ours and our competitors'?

- Were there particular areas we missed or identified missteps in the sales and/or buying process?

- What did the customer find most compelling about our offering or our messaging?

- Was the decision based on price? How did we compare to competitors' pricing?

Those questions often yield very illuminating answers. Most sellers are afraid of the answers; however, the highest performers want to know the details of why they lost. They don't let pride and ego get in the way of market intelligence.

The questions below similarly elicit important answers:

**Wins**

- Who were the relevant competitors?

- In addition to our company, who else made the final cut for further consideration? Why did they make the final cut?

- What were their perceived strengths compared with ours?

- Where did our presentations resonate most fully compared to those of our competitors? What were the most important strengths we communicated?

- What about our solution or our process created the biggest advantage for us in your mind?

- We appreciate being chosen to work with you. So that we can continue to grow in excellence, we'd also like to understand if there were any areas where we could have done a better job or represented ourselves in a better way. If so, please share.

It is far rarer for sellers to do debriefs with customers on why they win. Sellers tend to be so relieved that they won the deal, they just want to move on and enjoy the win. But taking even 30 minutes to have a post-decision debrief can yield significant insight.

## SUMMARY

Expertise is not a result of inherent traits or experience. Although these aspects appear to be contributors to expertise, the way individuals practice is the distinguishing factor that moves them beyond amateur to expert.

When individuals reach an acceptable level of competence, they often no longer strive for meaningful improvement. This is referred to as a state of *arrested development*. The only way to get beyond this plateau is through a type of practice called *deliberate practice*. Deliberate practice involves consistent practice at increasing levels of difficulty with immediate feedback. It involves pushing beyond an individual's comfort zone.

Experts develop mental models for better decision-making. They are able to shortcut the typical long process of analysis and quickly tap into reserves of learning to reach more quick and accurate decisions. The high quality of their decisions leads to better execution and improved performance over time. This high quality of mental models and good decision-making is true of experts in every field, including sales.

Another important activity that experts employ is the use of postmortems. They get very granular about why they win or lose, using that insight to drive further practice, better performance, and higher levels of expertise. Sales managers who incorporate postmortems into their coaching rhythms outperform managers who don't engage in this practice.

Deliberate practice, self-reflection, and postmortems all contribute to greater levels of sales expertise.

## *KEY TAKEAWAYS*

- Just because we have experience in sales doesn't mean we've achieved sales expertise.

- Once an acceptable level of skill is achieved, we often find ourselves in a state of arrested development, where continued improvement is not the goal.

- Experts continually challenge themselves to move beyond their comfort zone, desiring increased challenges as they continue to develop.

- Deliberate practice is a hallmark of expert performance, and it involves four primary elements:
    - A clear and specific goal
    - Performing tasks focused on that goal
    - Feedback
    - Pushing beyond the comfort zone for additional task execution

- Experts in every domain are good decision makers, using mental models to assist the speed and quality of their decisions.

- Sales enablement efforts should reflect deliberate practice, ensuring that sellers and sales managers have opportunities to practice tasks at increasing levels of difficulty with immediate feedback rather than relying on episodic, boot camp–style training.

CHAPTER **14**

# Gaining Precise Insights: The Role of Machine Learning

The focus of this chapter is to provide a path to increased under-standing and specificity regarding the current state of both sales management coaching and the buying situations salespeople face. Although it is true that much of this insight is particularly useful for sales and enablement leaders, salespeople can benefit greatly from these precise insights. If you are a seller, these insights can open your eyes to the possibilities for better understanding your customers and the sales approaches that win. If you are a leader, these insights will help point your sales coaching and enablement efforts in the right direction.

Most sales and sales enablement leaders want to replicate the actions and behaviors of their high performers, but many don't

239

know how. This is an ongoing and thorny problem because high performers are often unconsciously competent. High performers can't explicitly say why they perform at much higher levels than the rest of the team, and even when they try, observation supports that they are not accurate. Artificial intelligence (AI) is often seen as a potential solution to the problems that exist in identifying and replicating high-performer behavior.

> **High performers are often unconsciously competent. High performers can't explicitly say why they perform at much higher levels than the rest of the team.**

In the world of sales, AI tools and systems are all the rage. Salespeople use AI systems that analyze their sales calls and product pitches to determine which behaviors led to better outcomes. Coaching conversations can be analyzed using specific tags to determine coaching effectiveness, including relative talk time. If it can be captured or recorded, it can be analyzed using AI. Data abounds, yet insights do not always follow.

The goal of AI is to help salespeople and sales leaders make better decisions in the future based on behaviors exhibited in the past. It is a worthy goal; however, one of the challenges with AI is that if you don't tag the right things, the analysis you get may be faulty or misleading. In other words, for AI to be most effective, you must know what to look for and ensure that the AI system is able to recognize and analyze it.

Earlier in this book we detailed the research conducted on high-performing salespeople and sales managers. We've been able to codify those findings into specialized instruments we use to analyze relevant sales force data and compare it to high-performer practices. As ongoing research reveals new practices, those practices are incorporated into the instruments, improving the tools with each subsequent use. This enables us to keep our tools and techniques fresh and indicative of changes in high-performer behavior. And we continue to gather relevant data in a changing world and keep pace with new insights as they become available.

In this chapter, we will explore the ways we can gather data from salespeople and sales managers, compare those practices to research-based best practices, and give clients a status report on our findings that our clients can use in their sales organizations. We will examine the types of insights that can be gained using client data run through the lens of AI and *machine learning* using our AgileEdge® proprietary algorithm. We will explore how these insights can help equip and enable both salespeople and sales managers for success. We will examine which insights align to the different levels of agility, and how the highest-performing sellers and sales managers incorporate these insights into their daily practices.

## GAINING INSIGHTS FOR ORGANIZATIONAL AGILITY

Although organizational agility is primarily the domain of sales managers and leaders, there are instances in which salespeople must make decisions about aligning activities with results themselves. This process of ensuring that field-level execution is aligned with organizational goals is useful and relevant to all members of the sales force. When we've discussed organizational agility in prior chapters, we positioned it as the ability to ensure that field execution is aligned with organizational goals.

Since our goal is to equip sales managers to provide the best guidance and coaching, it is often important to understand the starting point before embarking on any enablement efforts for frontline sales managers. In other words, if we want to improve the sales managers' ability to make the best decisions regarding which activities their sellers should be executing, which type of coaching they should provide to sellers, and how to track leading indicators of success, it is useful to determine the type and level of current practices. This helps organizations determine whether current practices reflect desired practices, as well as where the biggest gaps are between what managers are currently doing versus what their organizations want them to be doing. This type of analysis answers this question:

> What are my sales managers currently doing, and how does high-performer behavior differ from everyone else?

We will examine each aspect of organizational agility and how machine learning can provide insights for future efforts.

## ALIGNING SALESPERSON EXECUTION AND MANAGER COACHING WITH ORGANIZATIONAL GOALS

To determine which objectives or key performance indicators (KPIs) sales managers are focused on now, and whether they are the ones organizational leaders want them to focus on, you can gather very detailed information on management coaching practices. By gathering and examining the relative focus of high-performing managers versus everyone else, you can get a sense for the degree to which managers are focused on different areas and the degree to which sales manager–reported practices align with seller-reported practices.

In essence, we take a very granular look in the rearview mirror and create a snapshot in time of how managers behave. The example in Figure 14.1 reflects a sample output for five different sales objectives and how high-performer behavior differs from everyone else.

| Objective Category | High Performers | Everyone Else |
|---|---|---|
| Existing products and services | 5.0 | 3.5 |
| New products and services | 4.0 | 3.0 |
| Cross-selling and up-selling | 3.0 | 4.0 |
| New customer type | 1.0 | 2.0 |
| Similar customer type | 2.5 | 2.0 |

FIGURE 14.1 **Focus of Sales Objectives and/or KPIs**
*Source:* VantagePoint Performance.

This analysis is quite useful, even in cases where high-performer behavior doesn't vary significantly from the rest of the pack. In Figure 14.1, you can see that although there aren't large variances between managers at different performance levels, it is glaringly obvious that none of the sales managers are focused on new customer acquisition. Why does this matter? Because if one of the company goals is increased market share, this lack of focus on new customer acquisition shows that management behavior is not focused on sales objectives that enable that growth. Alternatively, if existing account growth is the goal, these results align with that goal. Again, it gives organizational leaders a read on the degree to which manager behaviors align with organizational goals.

## IDENTIFYING SALES ACTIVITIES THAT MATTER MOST

The next question organizational leaders want to answer is this:

> Which activities are sellers focused on, and are they the ones sales leaders want them to focus on?

Using the same machine learning approach, sales manager activity can be analyzed to determine which seller activities they are focusing on and if high-performing managers' focus differs from that of everyone else. The machine learning algorithm can analyze which activities are positively and negatively associated with performance. In Figure 14.2, you can see which activities are positively associated with performance for one of our medical device clients. This chart illustrates the output of the analysis that examined over 25 different salesperson activities and isolated the ones most predictive of performance.

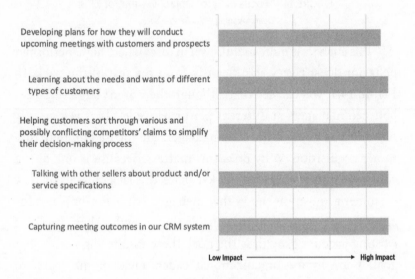

FIGURE 14.2 **Positive Performance Drivers: High-Impact Activities**
*Source:* VantagePoint Performance.

This information is often illuminating to organizational leaders. For example, in this case one of the high-impact activities, capturing meeting outcomes in the customer relationship management (CRM) system, is strongly and positively correlated with performance. This is not always the case; however, it was for this client. It provides further support of the importance of CRM system use and updates. In addition, planning for upcoming calls had a high impact, indicating that this is a behavior that managers want to encourage and coach to drive better performance.

It can also be interesting to note what is missing from this list of high-impact activities. This client had a heavy focus on account planning at the time of this analysis, yet not one account planning activity correlated with higher performance. This was alarming to this client, and it instigated a closer look at both the process and the adoption of the process. The client, with assistance, was able to determine why this disconnect existed and took steps to remedy the situation.

Figure 14.3 illuminates another problem with this client's sales management behavior. This is another example of a disconnect between existing versus desired sales manager behavior. Existing account growth was extremely important to this client.

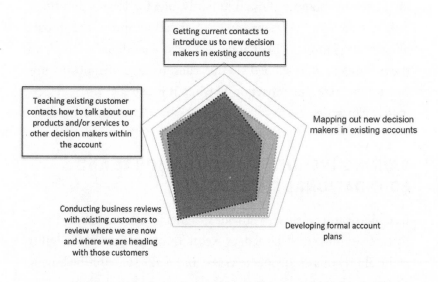

FIGURE 14.3 **Account Management Activities**
*Source:* VantagePoint Performance.

The analysis showed that sales managers had a high focus on account planning, which was in line with organizational goals. However, two of the account management activities vital to existing account growth were the lowest areas of focus for all managers. This client used this insight to help examine their current account planning process and accentuate account advocacy and referrals.

These types of insights are rarely gained by interviewing sales managers. A detailed accounting of current practices is required to generate these very specific insights. In addition to focusing on different types of activities, we can use this method to analyze how managers coach to these activities and whether current practices align with research-based best practices. In this case, sales managers were having short monthly meetings to discuss account plans. These meetings were only 30 minutes long.

From our research we know it is much more productive to conduct account planning less frequently, but for longer durations. This one small adjustment can dramatically improve the impact of account planning discussions. We have shared just a sample of the insights that are gained via this sales manager diagnostic process to illustrate the impact of AI when it is coupled with subject-matter expertise.

## GAINING INSIGHTS FOR SITUATIONAL AND FOUNDATIONAL SALES AGILITY

Machine learning can also provide insights for situational sales agility by examining deal-level data. Recall that situational sales agility is the ability of salespeople to assess and make sense of the buying situations they face, choose the sales approach with the best chance of a win, and then execute the appropriate tactics paying close attention to buyer reactions and changes in the buying situation. You may also recall that we referred to five categories of buying factors in prior chapters:

- Problem awareness

- Competitive landscape

- Customer dynamics

- Buying stage

- Solution definition

Each of these categories includes multiple buying factors. These five categories of buying factors are useful for teaching salespeople which types of information to seek, how to makes sense of the information they glean, and what that information means regarding the buying situation they face. Recall that the highest-performing salespeople adjust their sales approach to align to the buying situation they face. Machine learning is used to analyze individual deals across many salespeople to determine which factors within each category are most predictive of adjustments in seller behavior. Figure 14.4 indicates the buying factors with the most influence on salesperson behavior for one of our clients in the high-tech industry.

| Category | Buying Factor |
|---|---|
| Problem awareness | Business problems |
| Solution definition | Priority criteria |
| Customer dynamics | Potential departments |
| Competitive landscape | Number of competitors |
| Buying process | Initial stage of engagement |

FIGURE 14.4 **Most Influential Buying Factors**
*Source:* VantagePoint Performance.

Once the most important buying factors have been identified, we can then use machine learning to analyze the interaction of these factors and determine how they work together to form types of buying situations. In our research, most of our clients have between three and five types of buying situations. This can vary by business unit or geography.

As you can see in Figure 14.5, the buying factors for our high-tech client formed four types of buying situations. This gave sellers a snapshot of the most common buying situations they face as well as how the different factors line up in each situation.

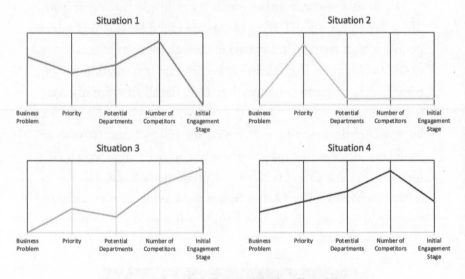

FIGURE 14.5 **Four Types of Buying Situations**
*Source:* VantagePoint Performance.

## IDENTIFYING SALES STRATEGIES THAT WIN

The next important pieces of information to glean are (a) which strategies and tactics are salespeople deploying in the different buying situations and (b) how likely is each one to lead to a win. As

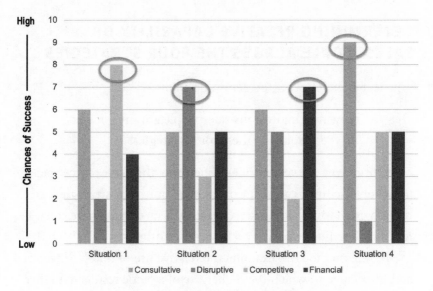

FIGURE 14.6  **Winning Strategies by Buying Situation**
*Source:* VantagePoint Performance.

you can see in Figure 14.6, all four sales strategies were being used by this client, and each of the four buying situations had a different optimal strategy. This is not always the case. Some of our clients have one strategy that is the best choice in more than one buying situation.

In Figure 14.6 you will notice that a disruptive (or challenging) strategy was only optimal in buying situation 2. This client had deployed the Challenger Sale and had seen limited success with the approach. This analysis helped the client understand why. It also pinpointed when a challenging style was optimal and when other approaches were more appropriate. It is highly unusual for one strategy to be optimal in all buying situations, further supporting the finding that the highest-performing sellers adapt their sales approaches to align to different buying situations.

## DETERMINING RELATIVE CAPABILITY OF SALESPEOPLE ACROSS THE FOUR STRATEGIES

The next question we often get is this one:

"How do I know if my salespeople are any good at
deploying these four strategies?"

Our clients are very curious about how their sales force stacks up when it comes to execution of the four sales strategies. Although evaluating salesperson capability is challenging, we can use machine learning to produce a few useful insights.

In one method, we examine the relative use of different tactics and the degree to which the higher use of a tactic results in higher win rates. Figure 14.7 reflects a client example of a relative heat map.

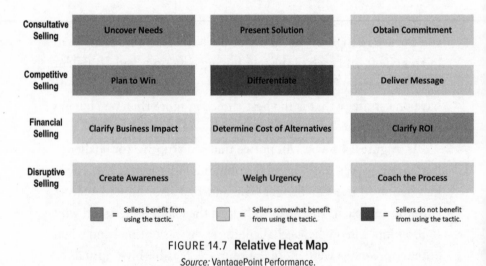

FIGURE 14.7  Relative Heat Map
*Source:* VantagePoint Performance.

To interpret Figure 14.7, we can draw the following conclusions:

- Sellers derive the biggest benefit from high use of (1) uncover needs, (2) present solutions, (3) plan to win, and

(4) clarify ROI. By benefit, what we mean is that when sellers use a higher amount of this tactic in deals, they have a better chance of winning. This does not mean the other tactics are unimportant. This interpretation has to do with the derived benefit from the higher use of a tactic.

- The higher use of other tactics is not necessarily beneficial. For example, the seven tactics in the lighter shade indicate that sellers receive some benefit from using the tactics, but it is not consistent. In addition, the higher use of the differentiate tactic is associated with losses. Again, this does not indicate whether one tactic is more important than another. It indicates that sellers get more benefit from the higher use of certain tactics than others.

## WHICH TACTICS MATTER MOST TO YOUR SALE?

Another question our clients often ask is this:

"Which tactics are most highly correlated with wins in my sales force?"

Answering that question requires a different type of analysis. To determine the answer to this question, we must examine the degree to which each tactic, when used at a moderate level, is correlated with wins. This analysis enables us to isolate the most critical tactics at the deal level for a given sales force. Figure 14.8 is an example of an *absolute heat map* for the same high-tech client in Figure 14.7. In this example of an absolute heat map, we see that differentiating, clarifying business impact, determining cost of alternatives, clarifying ROI, and creating awareness are all highly correlated with wins.

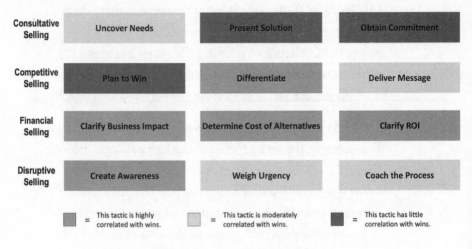

|  | | | |
|---|---|---|---|
| Consultative Selling | Uncover Needs | Present Solution | Obtain Commitment |
| Competitive Selling | Plan to Win | Differentiate | Deliver Message |
| Financial Selling | Clarify Business Impact | Determine Cost of Alternatives | Clarify ROI |
| Disruptive Selling | Create Awareness | Weigh Urgency | Coach the Process |

= This tactic is highly correlated with wins.   = This tactic is moderately correlated with wins.   = This tactic has little correlation with wins.

FIGURE 14.8 **Absolute Heat Map**
*Source:* VantagePoint Performance.

Insight comes when we compare the two analyses, and one insight quickly jumps to the surface. Salespeople receive the least benefit from using a high level of the differentiate tactic; however, the differentiate tactic is highly correlated with wins. This shows a gap between the relative capability of salespeople in this company to differentiate, and it shows the importance of differentiation to wins.

Other insights a sales leader might gain from these two heat maps is that (1) financial selling is critical to this sales force, (2) disruptive selling is also important, particularly creating awareness, and (3) the relative strengths of the sales force are not aligned with the tactics that are most critical to wins. This analysis highlights how important it is for salespeople to understand and be able to execute a variety of tactics across the four strategies versus choosing just one strategy such as consultative. These precise insights can be used to build out sales plays that increase the likelihood of a win in any given buying situation.

## EXAMINING CULTURAL DIFFERENCES IN STRATEGY USE

Our clients sometimes want to understand how cultural differences across regions affect strategy selection and use. When we examine deal-level data across regions, we often discover surprising findings. A very large global client requested an analysis of strategy selection by region. This client had strong opinions about the viability of certain strategy use, particularly in their Asia-Pacific region. The opinion was that the disruptive strategy would be particularly problematic in the Asia-Pacific region due to cultural norms. When we analyzed the regional breakdown for each buying situation, the client was shocked by the findings. The client had four types of buying situations, and the strategy use by region for situation 1 is shown in Figure 14.9.

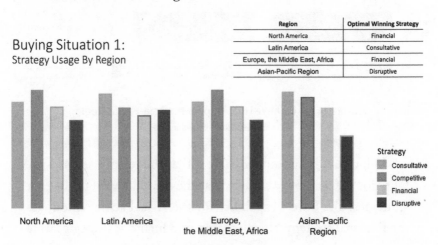

| Region | Optimal Winning Strategy |
| --- | --- |
| North America | Financial |
| Latin America | Consultative |
| Europe, the Middle East, Africa | Financial |
| Asian-Pacific Region | Disruptive |

**Buying Situation 1:**
Strategy Usage By Region

Strategy
- Consultative
- Competitive
- Financial
- Disruptive

North America    Latin America    Europe, the Middle East, Africa    Asian-Pacific Region

FIGURE 14.9 **Strategy Use by Region**
*Source:* VantagePoint Performance.

A few points to note are that the Asia-Pacific region was the only region that had the disruptive strategy as the optimal strategy for situation 1, although as Figure 14.9 indicates, it was the least used. Not only was this finding surprising, but the Asia-Pacific region was also the *only* region where the disruptive strategy was optimal for any of the four buying situations we analyzed.

When we examined relative seller capability by strategy for each region, we were in store for more surprises. Figure 14.10 shows the relative heat map for the Asia-Pacific region.

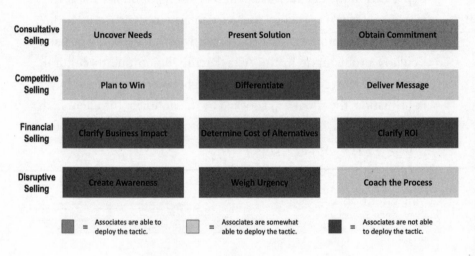

FIGURE 14.10  **Relative Heat Map for the Asia-Pacific Region**
*Source:* VantagePoint Performance.

What stands out immediately is that the relative seller capability for the disruptive strategy was the second lowest of the four strategies. The lowest capability for the Asia-Pacific region was the financial strategy. The disruptive and financial strategies were both optimal strategies for the buying situations we examined. This is a large skill gap in an area of strategic importance to the Asia-Pacific region. The use of the disruptive and financial strategies by the Asia-Pacific region, as well as the low relative seller capability to execute the tactics within these strategies, offered guidance on both training and coaching needs to properly equip the sales-people to recognize and effectively navigate the types of situations that buyers in this region faced.

## BUILDING OUT SALES PLAYS WITH HIGH PERFORMERS

With precise insights, organizations can work with high-performing sellers to build out specific sales plays for each buying situation based on the optimal sales approach identified. High-performing sellers examine each buying situation as well as the optimal sales approach most likely to lead to a win. They draw on their own ex-periences in similar situations, using specific tactics, to share what they do, say, and show as they execute tactics within the optimal strategy. The best tools and collateral to run each play are identified and codified into agility guides with specific and relevant guidance about what will most likely win for a given buying situation.

### SUMMARY

Sales and enablement leaders want reliable ways to identify and replicate high-performer behavior. Given the right algorithm, leaders can use AI and machine learning to identify these behaviors and practices at a granular level. These behaviors and practices can be replicated in sales and coaching plays for the rest of the orga-nization. In other words, this analysis identifies what your top per-formers do versus what the other 80 percent do, and you can then replicate that with the rest of the sales organization.

This level of precise insight can help sales leaders equip their sales force in a highly relevant way, but it also takes much of the guesswork out of sales enablement efforts. How do you know if you are making the right choices to enable your sales force? Let data be your guide. *Your* data, not someone else's. This dramatically reduces the risk associated with enablement decisions and increases the likelihood of high adoption and impact of those efforts, leading to greater impact on performance at all levels within the sales force.

> **How do you know if you are making the right choices to enable your sales force? Let data be your guide.**

## KEY TAKEAWAYS

- Sales and enablement leaders have a strong desire to understand and replicate high-performer behavior; however, most lack a reliable mechanism for accomplishing this task.

- Powerful insights from AI tools are highly dependent upon programming and tagging which behaviors represent desired performance.

- Machine learning can be used to do a deep, predictive analysis of current sales management and coaching practices to provide valuable insights regarding *organizational sales agility*:
  - Which sales objectives and KPIs are managers focused on, and how do high performers differ from everyone else?
  - Which activities receive the most focus, and which activities are correlated with higher performance?
  - How are high-performing sales managers coaching high-impact activities, and to what degree do current practices reflect research-based high-performer practices?

- Machine learning can be used to do deep, predictive analysis of current buying situations and sales strategies to provide valuable insights regarding *situational sales agility* to determine the following:
    - Which five to seven buying factors (among many) are the most highly influential of adaptations in seller behavior?
    - How do these high-influence buying factors cluster into types of company-specific buying situations?
    - Which sales strategies and tactics are being deployed in each buying situation, and which strategies are most predictive of wins and losses?
    - How do strategy selection and use vary by geographic region?
    - Which tactics among the four primary sales strategies are the most critical for sales within a specific sales force?
    - What are the sellers' relative capabilities for execution of each tactic within the four sales strategies?

- Once companies understand the nature of their company-specific buying situations and the sales strategies that win, they can then leverage their highest performers to build out sales plays that reflect what the highest performers do, say, and show in each type of buying situation.

# Appendix: Details of the Sales Agility Research Journey

## ORGANIZATIONAL AGILITY RESEARCH

### Sales Metrics Research, 2008 to 2010

University Sales Education Foundation and VantagePoint gather metrics data from 17 global sales organizations.

- Total number of metrics after elimination of duplicates: 306.

- The results, objectives, and activities (ROA) framework for measuring and managing a sales force was born.

- Published in our bestselling book *Cracking the Sales Management Code: The Secrets to Measuring and Managing Sales Performance*.

### Sales Coaching Study, 2017 to 2018

374 salespeople from a global manufacturing and services company. Formed the basis for Michelle Vazzana's PhD dissertation.

- Three types of coaching (capability, outcome, and activity) were examined regarding usage level and impact on quota attainment.

- *Punchline:* Activity coaching was the only type of coaching that was significantly and positively correlated with quota attainment. Which activities to coach? It depends. No one-size-fits-all answer.

### Sales Management and Coaching Practices Research, 2015 to 2017

Initial study: 518 managers from 12 global sales organizations. Examined sales coaching practices, sales role characteristics, and formal management rhythms.

- *Punchline:* No one best way to coach. Coaching is variable, and there is no one-size-fits-all way to do it. Patterns were identified that separate the top 25 percent of managers from the rest.

### Sales Management Coaching Practices Additional Research, 2017 to 2022

- Revalidated and expanded management practices and coaching research with 1,862 managers, 4,863 sellers, from 18 companies.

## SITUATIONAL AGILITY RESEARCH

### Florida State University (FSU) Sales Institute, Replication of Challenger Research, 2012

780 salespeople.

- Reps in the top 50 percent were more likely to identify themselves as challengers versus the bottom 50 percent.

- Reps in the top 25 percent were just as likely to identify themselves as consultative sellers.

- Reps in the bottom 50 percent were more likely to identify themselves as relational sellers.

**Situational Study, 2013**

1,500 salespeople from three different companies.

- High performers had a dominant selling style based on the situation they were asked to address.

- Average and low performers use the same approach regardless of the situation they face.

- High performers used a consultative style more than the other three strategies.

- Asking sellers what they "do" is very different and much more meaningful than asking them what they "are."

**Win Rate Study, 2014**

793 salespeople, three companies, 1,586 total sales opportunities analyzed.

- Each seller identified an opportunity they won and an opportunity they lost.

- Situational characteristics were identified as well as tactics deployed in the opportunity pursuit.

- Tactics used reflected the four patterns of sales behavior.

- Challenger-style selling was successful in only 4 of the 13 different situations analyzed.

- High performers were more likely to deploy the sales strategy with the best chances of winning compared with the rest of the sales organization. This pattern held true for all three companies participating in the study.

**VantagePoint Validation of FSU Situational Study, 2017 to 2019**

885 salespeople, 397 sales managers, nine companies, 1,770 opportunities analyzed.

- High-performing salespeople were the most likely to deploy the strategy with the greatest chance of a win in each buying situation.

- Four different sales strategies were deployed: consultative, disruptive, competitive, and financial.

- Consultative and competitive were the most prevalent.

- Between 5 and 7 buying factors (out of 25) were most predictive of adaptations in seller behavior, and these 5 to 7 factors were clustered to identify between four and six unique buying situations for each sales force.

## FOUNDATIONAL AGILITY RESEARCH

**VantagePoint Study of Buying Factors, 2020 to 2021**

4,196 opportunities reported by 2,098 sellers analyzed across seven companies to determine which buying factors were used most prevalently.

- Eight factors with very little use were eliminated, reducing dimensionality in the analysis. The 17 remaining factors formed five categories of buying factors that made up each unique buying situation.

- Although the number of unique buying situations varied, four types of buying situations were the most prevalent number per client.

- One buying factor (buying stage) was the only factor present and statistically significant in every sales opportunity, and it formed the foundation for the identification and understanding of all buying situations.

**VantagePoint Sales Tactics Study, 2021**

2,124 opportunities analyzed across 1,062 salespeople. Analysis determined how the use of the tactics within the four strategies related to one another.

- The four strategies were not as discrete as once believed. Although there were four patterns of sales tactics, a mixture of tactics from various strategies were deployed in each opportunity.

- The consultative tactics were deployed heavily in every opportunity regardless of which strategy was identified as dominant.

- Consultative tactics were deployed most heavily when the buying stage was early versus late. Consultative tactic usage in early-stage deals was six times higher than consultative tactic usage in late-stage deals.

- Consultative tactics were found to be necessary for determining the buying stage and determining whether to pivot to one of the other three strategies.

- Consultative tactics were foundational to strategy deployment and necessary to pivot to another strategy.

# Notes

**Introduction**

1. Michelle Vazzana and Leff Bonney, *Building an Agile Sales Organization: Moving Beyond the "How to" Mindset*, Sales Management Association Conference Archives, October 17, 2017, https://salesmanagement.org/search-page /?s=moving%2Bbeyond%2Bthe%2Bhow%2Bto%2Bmindset.
2. Alice Walmesley, "Reimagining the Unique Value-Add of the Seller with Situational Awareness," Gartner CSO and Sales Leader Conference, May 18, 2022.
3. Jason Jordan and Michelle Vazzana, *Cracking the Sales Management Code: The Secrets to Measuring and Managing Sales Performance* (New York: McGraw Hill, 2011).
4. Michelle Vazzana and Jason Jordan, *Crushing Quota: Proven Sales Coaching Tactics for Breakthrough Performance* (New York: McGraw Hill, 2018).
5. Carol Dweck, *Mindset: The New Psychology of Success* (New York: Random House, 2006).
6. K. Anders Ericsson, Robert R. Hoffman, Aaron Kozbelt, and A. Mark Williams, eds., *The Cambridge Handbook of Expertise and Expert Performance*, 2nd ed. (Cambridge, UK: Cambridge University Press, 2018), https://doi.org /10.1017/9781316480748.

**Chapter 1**

1. Megan Heuer, "Three Myths of the '67 Percent' Statistic," Forrester, blog, July 3, 2013, https://www.forrester.com/blogs/three-myths-of-the-67-percent -statistic/.
2. Nick Toman, "How Challenger Sales Organizations Should Make Sense of Sense Making," *Business Growth Strategies for Leaders* (blog), Gartner, June 27, 2019, https://blogs.gartner.com/nick-toman/how-challenger-sales-organiza tions-should-make-sense-of-sense-making/.
3. Ibid.
4. Eric Zines, "Five Questions to Ask Before Changing Sales Methodologies," Forrester, blog, September 25, 2020, https://www.forrester.com/blogs/five -questions-to-ask-before-changing-sales-methodologies/.

## Chapter 2

1. Alice Walmesley, "Reimagining the Unique Value-Add of the Seller with Situational Awareness," Gartner CSO and Sales Leader Conference, May 18, 2022.
2. Jason Jordan and Michelle Vazzana, *Cracking the Sales Management Code: The Secrets to Measuring and Managing Sales Performance* (New York: McGraw Hill, 2012).
3. Michelle Vazzana and Jason Jordan, *Crushing Quota: Proven Sales Coaching Tactics for Breakthrough Performance* (New York: McGraw Hill, 2018).
4. Michelle Vazzana and Leff Bonney, *Building an Agile Sales Organization: Moving Beyond the "How to" Mindset*, Sales Management Association Conference Archives, October 17, 2017, https://salesmanagement.org/search-page /?s=moving%2Bbeyond%2Bthe%2Bhow%2Bto%2Bmindset.
5. Matt Dixon and Brent Adamson, *The Challenger Sale: Taking Control of the Customer Conversation* (New York: Penguin Group, 2011).
6. The Challenger Sale is a registered trademark of Challenger, Inc., www.challengerinc.com.
7. Daniel Kahneman, *Thinking, Fast and Slow* (New York: Farrar, Straus and Giroux, 2011), pp. 302–303.
8. William Miller and Stephen Rollnick, *Motivational Interviewing: Helping People Change*, 3rd ed. (New York: Guilford Press, 2013), p. 6.

## Chapter 3

1. William Miller and Stephen Rollnick, *Motivational Interviewing: Helping People Change*, 3rd ed. (New York: Guilford Press, 2013), p. 3.
2. Ibid., p. 5.
3. Jonathan Haidt, *The Happiness Hypothesis: Finding Modern Truth in Ancient Wisdom* (New York: Basic Books, 2006), pp. 3–5.
4. Daniel Kahneman, *Thinking, Fast and Slow* (New York: Farrar, Straus and Giroux, 2011), pp. 302–305.
5. Ibid., pp. 303–304.

## Chapter 6

1. Robert Coram, *Boyd: The Fighter Pilot Who Changed the Art of War* (Boston: Little, Brown, 2002).
2. Ibid.
3. Mark Kelly, "The OODA Loop (Observe, Orient, Decide, Act): Applying Military Strategy to High-Risk Decision Making and Operational Learning Processes for On-Snow Practitioners," *Proceedings, International Snow Science Workshop*, Banff, Alaska, 2014, Heliskiing/AMGA, https://arc.lib.montana .edu/snow-science/objects/ISSW14_paper_P3.45.pdf.

4. Kevin Harris, "Why Former College Athletes Make Great Sales Pros," *Sales Development Blog*, memoryBlue, December 21, 2017, https://memoryblue .com/2017/12/why-former-college-athletes-make-great-sales-pros/.

## Chapter 7

1. Gaia Vince, "Cities: How Crowded Life Is Changing Us," *BBC Future*, May 16, 2013, https://www.bbc.com/future/article/20130516-how-city-life -is-changing-us.

## Chapter 9

1. Francesca Gino, "The Business Case for Curiosity," *Harvard Business Review*, September-October 2018, https://hbr.org/2018/09/the-business-case-for -curiosity#:~:text=Studies%20have%20found%20that%20curiosity,evaluated %20by%20their%20direct%20bosses.
2. K. Anders Ericsson, "Deliberate Practice and Acquisition of Expert Performance: A General Overview," *Academic Emergency Medicine*, Society for Academic Emergency Medicine, vol. 15, no. 11, November 3, 2008, pp. 988–992.
3. Justin Shinkle, Thomas W. Nesser, Timothy J. Demchak, and David M. McMannus, "Effect of Core Strength on the Measure of Power in the Extremities," *Journal of Strength and Conditioning Research*, vol. 26, no. 2, February 2012, pp. 373–380, doi: 10.1519/JSC.0b013e31822600e5 and PMID: 22228111, https://pubmed.ncbi.nlm.nih.gov/22228111/.
4. VantagePoint Performance, *Why Agile Salespeople Outperform Challengers: Situation-Based Strategies Win More Customers*.
5. Alice Walmesley, "Reimagining the Unique Value-Add of the Seller with Situational Awareness," Gartner CSO and Sales Leader Conference, May 18, 2022.
6. Brian Williams, "21 Mind-Blowing Sales Stats," Brevet Group, blog, https:// blog.thebrevetgroup.com/21-mind-blowing-sales-stats.

## Chapter 10

1. Nick Toman, "How Challenger Sales Organizations Should Make Sense of Sense Making," *Business Growth Strategies for Leaders* (blog), Gartner, June 27, 2019, https://blogs.gartner.com/nick-toman/how-challenger-sales-organiza tions-should-make-sense-of-sense-making/.

## Chapter 11

1. Eva Krockow, "How Many Decisions Do We Make Each Day?," *Psychology Today*, September 27, 2018, https://www.psychologytoday.com/us/blog /stretching-theory/201809/how-many-decisions-do-we-make-each-day; and Joel Hoomans, "35,000 Decisions: The Great Choices of Strategic Leaders," *Leading Edge*, Roberts Wesleyan College, March 20, 2015, https://go.roberts .edu/leadingedge/the-great-choices-of-strategic-leaders.

2. Ted Bauer, "The Neuroscience of Storytelling," *Your Brain at Work* (blog), NeuroLeadership Institute, September 30, 2021, https://neuroleadership .com/your-brain-at-work/the-neuroscience-of-storytelling/.

## Chapter 13

1. K. Anders Ericsson, Robert R. Hoffman, Aaron Kozbelt, and A. Mark Williams, eds., *The Cambridge Handbook of Expertise and Expert Performance*, 2nd ed. (Cambridge, UK: Cambridge University Press, 2018), https://doi .org/10.1017/9781316480748.
2. Ibid.
3. K. Anders Ericsson, "Deliberate Practice and Acquisition of Expert Performance: A General Overview," *Academic Emergency Medicine*, Society for Academic Emergency Medicine, vol. 15, no. 11, November 3, 2008, pp. 988–994.

# Index

Archetypes, 129–130, 133, 177–178, 184
Arrested development, 226
Artificial Intelligence (AI), 240, 256
Asia-Pacific region, 253–254
Assertive salesperson behavior, dislike of consumer of, 37, 50, 51, 155, 192
Assess, choose, execute process, 54, 152–161, 214–215, 218–219
Assessment, choice and, 152
Assessment of situation, 15, 33, 53–54, 120, 154–155
coaching of, 212–214
continuation of, 165–166
Associated skills, in coaching, 206
Assumptions, about buying process, 169–170, 176, 210, 233–234
Athletes, 105–106
Automated tasks, 224–225, 237
Awareness
of consumer problem, 55–57, 83, 122, 172
creation of, 187, 190

**B**

Background questions, 60, 81, 85, 188, 189
importance to sale of, 197
Ballet dancers, 152
Basic sales skills, 30
Benefit, to buyer, 74, 82, 86
Bias, 124–125, 176
Blind spot, of customer, 192
Bonney, Leff, 102
Bottom-line buyer, 130
Boyd, John, 100–101
"The Business Case for Curiosity" (Gino), 149
Buyer
benefit to, 74, 82, 86
concerns of, 211

emotions of, 41–42, 50
engagement of, 91
ideas preference for, 39–40, 50, 51, 210
perspective of, 125, 137
problem, 209–210
psychology of, 30, 38–39
responsiveness of, 67
situation assessment questions for, 60, 69
Buying
process, 55
signal, 213
stage consideration of, 123, 168–169
Buying factors
analysis of influential, 247–248, 257
categories for, 26–27, 54–55, 111, 121–122, 132, 155, 168–169, 180, 213–214, 247
Buying journey, 28, 30, 38–39, 45–47, 50, 55
coaching aligned to, 207–209
coaching on, 206–207
early stages of, 45–46, 59, 61, 88, 169
foundational agility and, 206–207
late stage of, 46–47, 66, 70, 169
mid stages of, 46, 63–64, 70, 82–83, 169
Buying situations, 25, 33, 53–54, 110, 116
archetypes of, 129–130, 133, 177–178, 184
combination of aspects of, 214
four types of, 248
information seeking and, 124–125
orienting and, 175–186
sales strategies and, 26
situational readiness and, 119–120

**C**

Careers, using agility, 102
Case studies, 9–10

GOAT. *See* Greatest of all time
Golf, 150
   sales compared with, 224–226
Greatest of all time (GOAT), 105

**H**

Habit
   conscious decision-making versus,
     143
   experience and, 150
Haidt, Jonathan, 42
*Harvard Business Review* (magazine),
   149
High performers, study of, 9–10, 11,
   12, 13–14, 33
   artificial intelligence and, 240–241
   in coaching, 20–21
   deliberate practice and, 232
   replication of performance of, 239,
     255, 256
   use of different strategies by, 25,
     120, 182
High-impact activity
   coaching for, 202, 219–220, 245, 256
   positive performance drivers and,
     244
High-quality decisions, performance
   and, 230–231, 236
Hooks, for retention of information,
   191
House buying example, 47–49, 64–65
House criteria, 48
House inspection, risk mitigation
   and, 49

**I**

Ideas of buyers, preference for, 39
Immediate feedback, 229–230
Important aspects, narrowing down
   of, 46
Incorrect hypotheses, research and,
   13–14

Incremental commitments,
   obtainment of, 30–31, 34, 76
Indicators, monitoring of, 21–22, 32,
   219
Information
   application of, 118–119
   consolidation of, 175–176, 186–187
   overload, 3–5, 8–9, 11, 118
   process of providing, 75
   seeking of, 80, 84, 94, 124–125, 155
   sharing of, 80, 84, 89–90, 94
Initial engagement, with customer,
   27–28
Input, in coaching session, 203, 221
   planned review of, 204
Insight, 4–5, 12
   from machine learning, 245–246
Intelligence
   readiness and, 148
   shortage of, 118
Internally gathered data, 177
In-the-moment coaching, planned
   coaching versus, 202–203

**J**

Jordan, Michael, 158
Junior team member, keynote speech
   and, 129

**K**

Kahneman, Daniel, 42, 44–45
Key performance indicators (KPIs),
   18, 242
Keynote speech, junior team member
   and, 129
KPIs. *See* Key performance indicators

**L**

Late stage, of buying journey, 46–47,
   66, 70, 169
   importance of coaching before,
     211–212

Targeted ads, 3
Technology, indirect consequences
of, 4
Technology revolution, 4, 8–9, 12
Therapist example, 40–41
Time, 20, 108
Tool choice, as cyclical, 142
Toolkit, of effective salesperson, 114
Tools, rules versus, 110–112, 186
Training, in decision-making, 232
Triage nurse, knowledge of, 104–105
Turning point, in story arc, 195

**U**

Unconscious biases, 126
Unresponsiveness, 67–68
Urban apartment, 48

**V**

VantagePoint, 17, 110, 130, 133, 145
research of, 202, 204–205
resources of, 177–178, 180, 187,
198
Varied toolkit, 136
Vazzana, Michelle, 150
Vision, of consumer, 171

**W**

Weightlifting, 154
Williams, Serena, 105–109
Willingness to engage, 123
Winning sales strategies,
248–249
Winning strategies, 249
Wins, questions for, 235